ANCIENTS AND MODERNS

General Editor: Phiroze Vasunia, Reader in Classics, University of Reading

How can antiquity illuminate critical issues in the modern world? How does the ancient world help us address contemporary problems and issues? In what ways do modern insights and theories shed new light on the interpretation of ancient texts, monuments, artefacts and cultures? The central aim of this exciting new series is to show how antiquity is relevant to life today. The series also points towards the ways in which the modern and ancient worlds are mutually connected and interrelated. Lively, engaging, and historically informed, *Ancients and Moderns* examines key ideas and practices in context. It shows how societies and cultures have been shaped by ideas and debates that recur. With a strong appeal to students and teachers in a variety of disciplines, including classics and ancient history, each book is written for non-specialists in a clear and accessible manner.

ALFRED S. BRADFORD holds the John Saxon Chair of Ancient History at the University of Oklahoma. He served in Vietnam in 1968–9 as an Infantry Officer with the First Battalion, Twenty-Seventh Infantry Regiment ('First Wolfhounds') and wrote a memoir about his experiences – *Some Even Volunteered*. He is also the author of *A Prosopography of Lacedaemonians from the Death of Alexander the Great, 323 B.C., to the Sack of Sparta by Alaric, A.D. 396*; *Philip II of Macedon*; *With Arrow, Sword, and Spear: A History of Warfare in the Ancient World*; *Flying the Black Flag: A Brief History of Piracy*; and *Leonidas and the Kings of Sparta: Mightiest Warriors, Fairest Kingdom*.

ANCIENTS AND MODERNS SERIES

ANCIENTS AND MODERNS

WAR
ANTIQVITY AND
ITS LEGACY

ALFRED S. BRADFORD

OXFORD
UNIVERSITY PRESS

OXFORD
UNIVERSITY PRESS

Oxford University Press is a department of the University of Oxford. It furthers the University's
objective of excellence in research, scholarship, and education by publishing worldwide.

Oxford New York
Auckland Cape Town Dar es Salaam Hong Kong Karachi
Kuala Lumpur Madrid Melbourne Mexico City Nairobi
New Delhi Shanghai Taipei Toronto

With offices in
Argentina Austria Brazil Chile Czech Republic France Greece
Guatemala Hungary Italy Japan Poland Portugal Singapore
South Korea Switzerland Thailand Turkey Ukraine Vietnam

Oxford is a registered trademark of Oxford University Press in the UK
and certain other countries.

Published in the United States of America by
Oxford University Press
198 Madison Avenue, New York, New York 10016

www.oup.com

First published by I.B.Tauris & Co. Ltd in the United Kingdom

A copy of this book's Cataloging-in-Publication Data is on file with the Library of Congress

ISBN (HB): 978-0-19-538090-3
ISBN (PB): 978-0-19-538091-0

Typeset in Garamond Pro by Ellipsis Digital Limited, Glasgow
Printed and bound in Great Britain by CPI Group (UK) Ltd, Croydon, CR0 4YY

To my wife, Pam

CONTENTS

Map 1: Ancient Italy

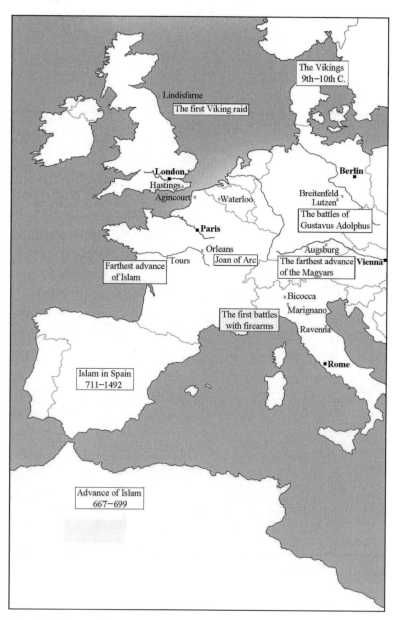

The Vikings
9th–10th C.

Lindisfarne
The first Viking raid

London

Berlin

Hastings
Agincourt
Waterloo

Breitenfeld
Lutzen

The battles of
Gustavus Adolphus

Paris

Orleans
Joan of Arc

Tours

Augsburg
The farthest advance
of the Magyars

Vienna

Farthest advance
of Islam

Bicocca
Marignano

Ravenna

The first battles
with firearms

Islam in Spain
711–1492

Rome

Advance of Islam
667–699

Map 2: Western Europe

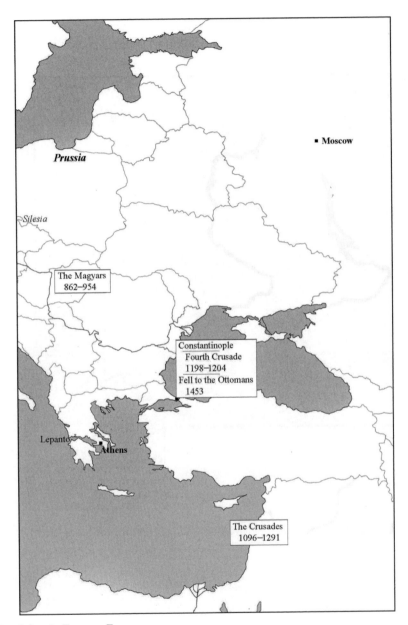

Map 3: Eastern Europe

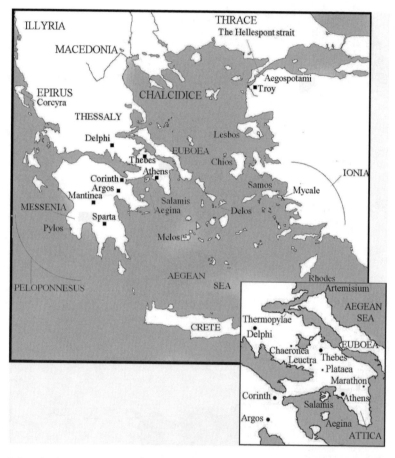

Map 4: Ancient Greece (with insert showing significant battle sites)

FOREWORD

Ancients and Moderns comes to fruition at a propitious moment: 'reception studies' is flourishing, and the scholarship that has arisen around it is lively, rigorous, and historically informed; it makes us rethink our own understanding of the relationship between past and present. *Ancients and Moderns* aims to communicate to students and general readers the depth, energy, and excitement of the best work in the field. It seeks to engage, provoke, and stimulate, and to show how, for large parts of the world, Greco-Roman antiquity continues to be relevant to debates in culture, politics, and society.

The series does not merely accept notions such as 'reception' or 'tradition' without question; rather, it treats these concepts as contested categories and calls into question the illusion of an unmediated approach to the ancient world. We have encouraged our authors to take intellectual risks in the development of their ideas. By challenging the assumption of a direct line of continuity between antiquity and modernity, these books explore how discussions in such areas as gender, politics, race, sex, and slavery occur within particular contexts and histories; they demonstrate that no culture is monolithic, that claims to ownership of the past are never pure, and that East and West are often connected together in ways that continue to surprise and disturb many. Thus, *Ancients and Moderns* is intended to stir up debates about and within reception studies and to complicate some of the standard narratives about the 'legacy' of Greece and Rome.

All the books in *Ancients and Moderns* illustrate that *how* we think about the past bears a necessary relation to *who* we are in the present. At the same time, the series also seeks to persuade scholars of antiquity that their own pursuit is inextricably connected to what many generations have thought, said, and done about the ancient world.

Phiroze Vasunia

PREFACE

'War is the father of all things' – Heraclitus[1]

One evening in 1969 I was sitting on a bunker in a fire support base in Vietnam. I was listening to our artillery shoot interdicting fire, and I was thinking about where I was, why I was there and, really, how different it would have been to be with Caesar in Gaul. I was a soldier in a fortified camp in hostile territory surrounded by the enemy. His soldiers, too, occupied fortified camps in hostile territory surrounded by the enemy. In the barest terms we, like them – even though technology had changed dramatically – were still endeavouring to drive chunks of metal into the flesh of our enemies and our enemies were trying to do the same to us.[2] I have to add that we were firing our artillery under a full moon while on that moon at that moment – I am not making this up – Americans were taking their first steps. What strange beings we are, I thought, that we are both up there – spiritually and physically – and down here, and I reflected on how much in 2,000 years has changed, and, stranger still, how much has not changed. Our fire support base would easily be recognised by a Roman soldier as a military camp, as we would recognise his and, furthermore, even across that space of time, I doubted that our visceral reaction to combat would be much different.

By one estimate, in the last 5,000 years human beings have fought wars 94 years of every hundred.[3] In my own lifetime of approximately three score and ten, the United States has been involved in 30 years' worth of wars, not counting the years of the Cold War nor those wars in which the United States had an interest, but had not committed regular armed forces. I, personally, spent one year of my life plus a couple of summers training, and another year in combat.

War is a part of our lives today and it has been a part of our lives at least as long as records have been kept … and undoubtedly much longer. We read the accounts of ancient warfare for many reasons: military officers to study strategy and tactics and broaden their education; historians to answer questions of causation and event; philosophers to consider questions concerning the morality of war; and the general public to be informed and, perhaps, as an unfortunate part of human nature, to be entertained. Fundamentally, we study ancient warfare to learn about ourselves.

INTRODUCTION

A work on war in a series entitled *Ancients and Moderns* must be concerned with the continuities and similarities between the past and the present, must be concerned with the extent to which modern warfare, in all its aspects including morality and law, has been directly influenced – and defined – by ancient warfare and, finally, it must be concerned with the realities of war, for war of any period imposes its own reality. Soldiers are afraid. Some become heroes, some run away. Some are leaders, most are followers. Some commit horrific acts, some are the victims of horrific acts. All are changed by their experience.

Our first task, simple enough it would seem, is to define war but, when we consult a few dictionaries, we encounter different definitions and we uncover a debate reaching back to Cicero. The *Oxford English Dictionary* defines war as a 'hostile contention by means of armed forces carried on by nations, states, or rulers'. This definition is essentially the same as Cicero's. The *New Oxford American Dictionary* defines war as 'a *state* of armed conflict between different nations or states'. This definition is essentially the definition of Hugo Grotius (*fl.* 1625) who rejected Cicero's definition, because war is a *condition* and not a *contest*.[1] International lawyers and diplomats prefer the latter definition, while the general public thinks of war more as Cicero did.

Now, if the very definition of war involves a discussion reaching back 2,000 years, what of the concepts of modern war? The vocabulary of war, to be sure, derives from Greek and Latin – army, military, strategy, tactics

1

– and our metaphors evoke the weapons of ancient times: 'live by the sword and die by the sword' does not seem dated in the way that, say, 'live by the musket and die by the musket' might. 'Sword' is used frequently to denote combat, as 'to draw the sword', and the 'Roman sword' seems to present a particularly graphic image. When the neurosurgeon, Babu Welch, emphasises the dangers of the improper use of a catheter, he tells his class that, improperly used, it will cut the patient 'like a Roman sword'.

Some modern military historians believe that our concepts of waging war – that war is won by fighting and winning a series of battles – derive directly from the Greeks and Romans. We emphasise battle, they say, because the Romans emphasised battle, the Romans emphasised battle because the Greeks did, and the Greeks emphasised battle partly because of Greek realities – the peculiarities of their political organisation and their topography – and partly because of an intellectual literary tradition beginning with the *Iliad*.

These historians point out that modern Western and Eastern concepts of war differ because they come from different traditions. They compare the practice of war in the West to the game of chess and the practice of war in the East (based on the philosophy of Sun Tzu that the best leader wins without fighting a battle) to the game of *Go*.[2]

The question of the origins and causes of our concept of war is not only interesting in itself, but has major implications for our own armed forces and the way we fight wars. Was the slaughter of World War I due to a narrow concept of how to fight a war? Did the United States fail in Vietnam because of a flawed strategy, based on western concepts? Did the Japanese learn western concepts of war and so adopt an unwinnable strategy in China and a disastrous strategy in the Pacific?

The quintessential Marine officer in World War II, Chesty Puller, served in the battle for Guadalcanal, a campaign which hardly resembled any campaign in the ancient world, and yet Caesar was there. Puller kept Caesar's *Gallic Wars* in his pocket and reread it so often that he went through several copies. He was inspired by the personal example of Caesar and he consciously followed one of his precepts – when he stopped for the night, he fortified.

For his part, Caesar would have recognised the Marine division as a military unit and, if the equipment and tactics were unfamiliar, still everything else – organisation, supply, chain of command, medals for bravery, the wearing of uniforms – would have been recognisable.

We can trace five paths of influence from Julius Caesar and the legions of Rome down to Chesty Puller and the modern military: 1) military terminology, 2) textbooks which draw on tactics and strategy from the ancient world, 3) the organisation of the military, 4) the evolution of weapons, and 5) directly, through Caesar's extant (translated) works and the works of other ancient authors. Caesar, in his turn, looked back to Alexander the Great while Alexander looked back to the *Iliad*.

The concepts of warfare are perhaps the most important legacy from the past, but not the only one. We can hold in our hands a Spartan shield, a Roman sword and coins the Athenians used to pay their oarsmen. We can look at detailed ancient representations of a Greek hoplite or a Roman soldier in action. We have papyri written in the ancient world and we have texts surviving, copy by copy, from that time to this. We can read them in the original languages, if we wish, or in translation.

All these are our legacy, but the most striking legacy of all is the *Iliad*.

CHAPTER I

THE *ILIAD*: WARFARE IN THE AGE OF HOMER

The *Iliad* is the first work of western literature, the first work of war literature, and the only work from classical antiquity that describes individual combat, individual feelings in combat and the fine balance between heroism and cowardice. The *Iliad* remains the premier literary work of war. (That it is also the premier work of all literature can by no means be dismissed.) The *Iliad* is itself a legacy, a book we can hold in our hands and read.

The *Iliad* influenced every generation of Greeks in the ancient world from its composition in the eighth century down to the fall of the Byzantine Empire in 1453. In the West it captivated Romans – and inspired Virgil to write the *Aeneid* (and later Stephen Vincent Benet to write *John Brown's Body*) – but the *Iliad* was lost in the West after the fall of the Roman Empire and its subject, the Trojan War, was known only through the tradition of two lesser authors (Dictys Cretensis and Daros of Phrygia). The *Iliad,* brought to Italy in the early 1400s, first appeared in English translation (by Arthur Hall) in 1581 and then in the seminal and influential translation of George Chapman (1611).[1] From that day to this, it has never been out of print and, as a rule, has been retranslated in every generation (sometimes more than once – in America recently by Richmond Lattimore, Robert Fagles and Steven Mitchell), it has never been given a bad review and it still sells well in multiple languages. Even as I wrote this paragraph, the New York Theater Workshop was presenting a one-man show, *The*

Iliad, 'illuminating both the heroism and the horrors of warfare'. The reviewer writes, 'A cracking good yarn it certainly is'.[2]

The *Iliad* relates an episode in a brief period of the tenth year of the Trojan War. Achilles quarrels with Agamemnon, withdraws from the fighting, returns to avenge the death of his friend Patroclus and fights and kills the principal champion of Troy, Hector.

The *Iliad* describes primitive warfare (in the technical sense), but the psychology is exact, and the participants are distinct individuals with striking personalities (unlike the earlier *Epic of Gilgamesh* and the later Indian epic, the *Mahabharata*). The *Iliad* is a deep, sophisticated work of literature in which readers can find the glory or the pathos of war, depending on what they themselves bring to the epic. Every reading of the *Iliad* reveals something new. Every soldier can find himself in the *Iliad*. It depicts wounds accurately and does not minimise the brutality of war nor the advantages of peace. Part of the uniqueness of the *Iliad* is that we, the readers, learn the names of the slain, their antecedents and often also the family who will mourn them; for instance, Axylos (killed by Diomedes), the son of Teuthras was (vi 12ff) 'well-loved; he lived a prosperous life in pleasant Arisbe, a friend to all who passed on the road by the house where he lived, but none of them was present to save him from tearful destruction'.

In the *Iliad* we have a complete picture of war: gore, brutality, loss, tenderness and love, and an answer to the question: if war is so brutal and dangerous, why go into combat at all? Sarpedon, the son of Zeus, explains it to his friend (xii 309–28):

Glaucus, why are we two honoured most of all in Lycia with the best seats and cuts of meat and full cups, and all look upon us as gods and we have large plots of fertile land by the banks of the Xanthus River and beautiful orchards and wheat-bearing fields – is it not because we are the first among the Lycians to go into battle and throw ourselves into the maelstrom of war so that someone of the stoutly armoured Lycians would say.

'It is just ... because our kings fight in the front ranks.'

But, my friend and companion, if we two, by fleeing this battle, could always live without sorrow or death, I would not go into the front ranks. Alas, ten thousand ways of death stand over us and it is not for mortals to flee them or avoid them, so let us go and seize glory from someone or perhaps give it to another.

This speech explains the code by which heroes live, but it also makes clear that life, if it were not limited, would be sweeter even than honour. Achilles, the most heroic of heroes, expresses the same opinion, but ... 'the generations of men are no more than the generations of leaves; the winds pour the leaves on the ground, but the trees in their new growth display others in the season of spring' (ix 401–2; vi 146–9).

The only immortality we can attain is the honour we win in life.

Men are mortal but the gods are not, and in the *Iliad* the gods are the primary movers of events: Apollo's anger that his priest was mistreated by Agamemnon creates the situation in which Achilles and Agamemnon quarrel, although Achilles' fury is part of his personality and he needs no urging from a god to express it; indeed, he would have drawn his sword and attacked Agamemnon if Athena had not caught him by the hair and pulled him back.

The gods act for personal reasons completely familiar to human beings. In stark contrast to the army assembly, they gather for dinner on Mount Olympus (viii 1–27, 198–211) very much like a contemporary human family. Zeus, because of a debt he owed to Thetis (the beautiful sea-goddess and mother of Achilles) and also because he was susceptible to her beauty, has acceded to her plea to avenge the insult to her son. His decision has angered his wife, Hera, and his daughter, Athena, who berate him for his decision and for helping Hector. In his position as father and husband, he threatens to use force, if he must, to compel them to obey him. Athena is chastened but, like any daughter confident in her relationship with her father, says that he will soon again be calling her his 'darling, grey-eyed girl' (viii 373). Hera, on the other hand, no match for Zeus physically, sets out to seduce him, using the magical bra of lust (xiv 214–7), borrowed from

Aphrodite – it drives sane males, men and gods, mad. Zeus takes one look at Hera, dressed up, and longs for her more, he says, than any other of his conquests – and he names them! Afterwards Hera and Sleep cast Zeus into a deep slumber, so Hera can slip away and help the Achaeans (xiv 312–55). The word of Zeus among gods and men may be supreme but he can be outmanoeuvred, and he, himself, is subject to a greater force ... Fate.

Because men believed that they were controlled by fate and by the gods, they considered courage and fear to be attributes now granted to some and now taken away. Success in battle depended upon the prowess of the hero, certainly, but also upon his standing in the divine world and, ultimately, upon his fate. To retreat was not necessarily a disgrace but simply an aspect of divine activity – although cowardice was recognised and condemned.

In the first 400 lines of the *Iliad* Homer sets forth all the issues: the anger of Achilles; honour; rivalry; the will and personal role of the gods; Zeus the father and husband and his relationship with his wife, Hera; family dynamics; personalities; the weakness and futility of Agamemnon; the influence of Achilles in the assembly and with the gods; army morale; the personal relationships between some gods and some men and between man and man; strife personified (Eris); plague; the nature of command and the corruption of power; human mortality; the suffering of the soldiers; the nature of siege warfare; looting and wealth; the ego, heroism and cowardice; the emotions; and the individual motives for going to war – Achilles for one had no personal grievances against the Trojans, but he 'longed for the war cry and battle'. Homer delineates the two worlds of men and gods and the role of the seer in observing and interpreting the divine world (i 492).

The seer treads a dangerous path. He looks into the divine world and he reports to kings, but the kings (in this case, Agamemnon) do not necessarily like what he tells them, even if they do believe him, and they should believe him because, without the help of a seer, human beings can have no certainty in the interpretation of signs. In Book II (1–34) Agamemnon has a dream sent by Zeus, but the dream is false, sent to deceive him.

Agamemnon, however, decides, without consulting an expert, that the dream is true, and on this basis he tests his army by suggesting that they all go home. The army fails the test miserably and rushes for the ships: Agamemnon is at a complete loss.

The king's failure to accede to the advice of the seer or to seek an interpretation of his dream are characteristics of a far-from-perfect king, but Agamemnon has been given the sceptre by Zeus and, therefore, he *is* king, even with his flaws: he is self-centred, greedy, slow to take personal risks, quick to take offence and of suspect judgement, but he does command a prickly bunch, as quick to take offence as he is. When he chides a noble, he chooses his words with care (or he risks getting backtalk or worse); when he chides a common man, he is free (as are the other nobles) to use force. His army comprises the aristocratic leaders (lesser kings) and their followers, who are personally loyal to their own 'kings' and have come to Troy in obedience to them. Agamemnon must persuade the aristocrats to follow him and then their retainers will follow them. Agamemnon could never appeal over Achilles' head to the Myrmidons. When the army meets in assembly, they meet to hear what their leaders have to say, not to debate the issues.

After Odysseus – and other heroes – restore order and summon the army back to assembly, Agamemnon describes the battle that is to come (the first in the *Iliad*): a battle to be fought until dark, in which the men's hands will sweat on their spears and on their shield straps while they themselves, and their horses, too, will be soaked with sweat (ii 385–90). Each man, as he prepared to enter the battle (ii 401), prayed to escape the death dealt by Ares.

And in the heart of each arose the desire for battle and for war; for them war had become sweeter than their return in the hollow ships to their beloved native land [. . .] and the gleam of the bronze reached up to heaven. (ii 450ff)

But first they eat and drink, because, as Odysseus says (xix 225–6, 231–2), 'We do not grieve for the dead with our stomachs, for when would we stop our fasting, if we did? [...] We must remember food and drink to be all the stronger to battle the enemy'.

Agamemnon and Hector realise that the coming battle will be so ferocious, so full of suffering and death, that they try to avert it by arranging a duel between Menelaus and Paris. The preparations for the duel take up almost the whole of Book III – the oaths, some digressions to give more of a description of Menelaus and, finally, the sacrifices. Agamemnon 'slit the throats of the lambs with the pitiless bronze and they fell to the ground gasping, losing their lives' (iii 293f). So, too, might the man who loses this duel fall gasping to the ground.

The two sides measure out the field, supervise the drawing of lots, and then the two combatants arm themselves. Arming is one of the standard scenes in literature and art. The warrior is variously shown putting on each piece of equipment: his greaves, his breastplate and helmet; picking up his shield; and hefting his spear. After donning his armour he moves in it to determine that it fits properly (xix 385–6) and then the two combatants advance to the duelling ground.

This duel should hold no surprises. Menelaus is by far the better warrior, he has justice on his side and he is certain to win, unless, that is, a god intervenes. Paris throws his spear first and hits Menelaus' shield but cannot penetrate it. Then Menelaus throws his spear and it pierces Paris' shield and his breastplate and the linen underneath, but Paris swerves and avoids the point. Menelaus draws his sword, rushes forward and strikes Paris on the helmet, but the sword shatters into half-a-dozen pieces. Menelaus drops the sword and seizes Paris by the crest of his helmet and starts to drag him to the Greek side. Aphrodite breaks the helmet strap. Menelaus picks up a spear to finish Paris off and Aphrodite wraps Paris in a cloud of dense air and whisks him away to the arms of Helen ... who is not so happy to see him:

So you are back from the duel! You ought to have died there,
Killed by a mightier man, who once in the past was my husband
   [...]

He is better far than you in the strength of his hand and spear
  (iii 428–31)

Paris replies that Menelaus won because he had Athena to help him (which
the reader knows to be untrue but which, nonetheless, is plausible). Paris,
however, is a man who is ever ready to find an excuse for himself. And he
goes on to tell her that he wants her, and that he had never wanted her
more (iii 442), which is another instance of Homer's keen insight into
human psychology – the affirmation of life through sex after a close call.

Book IV begins with Athena convincing the archer Pandarus to break
the truce by firing an arrow at Menelaus, and then Athena turns the arrow
aside slightly, so that it penetrates the armour of Menelaus and the linen
underneath, but makes only a shallow wound (iv 140ff). The duel has not
settled the issue, but rather has inflamed it, and both sides marshal for
battle. (As always in the *Iliad*, the situation is ambiguous – is the violation
of an oath a moral wrong when it has been instigated by a god?)

Later, in Book VII, Homer describes how honourable men conduct a
duel. Hector issues a challenge. Menelaus prepares to accept it and arms
himself, but is held back by Agamemnon because Hector is by far the
stronger warrior in 'battle where men win glory' (iv 113). Nestor has to
shame the reluctant Achaean heroes into volunteering. Aias is chosen by
lot, he strides forth to fight the duel, and Hector feels a bit of fear upon
seeing him (iv 235ff): Aias and Hector confront each other, Aias boasts
about his own prowess and Hector replies:

I, myself, understand battle where men are slain
I know how to swing my shield now to the right, and now to
  the left,
And I know all the steps to use on the dancing-floor of Ares.

They each cast one of their spears and then they fight with the other.
Aias wounds Hector in the neck. Hector picks up a rock and hurls it at
Aias and Aias retaliates with a bigger rock, which strikes Hector's shield.

The shield crumples and Hector falls to the ground. Apollo brings him to his feet again and the two heroes are about to continue the duel with swords, but the herald intervenes because both have amply proved their prowess and courage, and also because night is falling. Hector agrees, as the challenger, and the two exchange gifts and part friends. This is the way honourable men fight a duel.

Agamemnon goes the rounds of his army (iv 223ff), praising and encouraging those who are preparing for battle – 'vultures will feed on the flesh of the oath-breakers and we will carry off their wives and dear little children in our ships' – but when he sees some men shirking their duty he berates them and compares them to fawns which run across the plain and then stop when they are tired 'because they have no strength in their hearts' (iv 242–3). Not everyone in the *Iliad* is a hero, not everyone is eager for battle and, sometimes, even the heroes themselves are unwilling to enter into combat.

Agamemnon visits the leaders and he praises or criticises them depending on their enthusiasm. He praises the Cretan Idomeneus, the two Aiantes and Nestor, who has arranged his army with the chariots in front, his finest troops in the rear and the rest – the hesitant or suspect – in the middle where they will have no choice but to advance. Agamemnon encounters Odysseus who appears to be holding back – because he has received no orders – and chides him for his hesitancy. Odysseus glowers at him and says (iv 350), 'What nonsense you talk, son of Atreus!' Agamemnon immediately backs down. Next he comes upon Diomedes and unfairly criticises him for not going into battle. Diomedes accepts the unjust rebuke because he acknowledges that Agamemnon is his superior.

The two armies advance.

Ares encouraged one side, Athena the other and Dread and Rout were there and raging Eris, the man-slaying sister and companion of Ares. She appears first as a little thing, but, as she casts hatred between the two armies, going in the throng and being responsible for the dying groans of men, then she strides upon the earth and she strikes the heavens with her head. (iv 439–45)

(The portrait of Eris [Strife] in the *Iliad* is psychologically apt – men hesitate at the beginning but, as they are infused with adrenalin, they forget about themselves and plunge wholeheartedly into battle.)

The Greek ranks press on, officers calling to the men, the men silent, until the two armies meet.

'They clashed their arms together, and their spears, these mighty bronze-clad men [...] and they smashed the bosses of their shields together and a great din arose and here and there vaunts and screams of those who were killing and those who were being killed. Blood flowed on the ground. (iv 446ff)

The struggle became a general melee. Antilochus (a Greek) struck Echopolus (a Trojan) on the ridge of the helmet over the forehead. The point penetrated the bone and he dropped dead. A Greek warrior tried to drag the body from the melee by the feet to strip him of his armour, but he exposed his side and a Trojan stabbed him there and killed him. The two sides fought over the bodies 'like wolves; they rushed on each other and fought man to man' (iv 471–2).

Then Aias killed Simoisius. Simoisius had been named for the river Simois besides which he had been conceived. 'His life was too short for him to repay his parents for their loving care' (iv 478). The spear went in above the right nipple and came out the shoulder in the back.

Odysseus made a cast of his spear and killed a man and the Trojans fell back. Apollo called upon the Trojans to remember that the Achaeans were not made of metal or stone, that bronze would penetrate their flesh while, on the other side, Athena urged on anyone who held back. The combatants suffered horrible wounds – a leg shattered by a rock, a sword in the belly, a spear in the lungs, a spear thrust in the belly. Intestines spilled on the ground – a common result of a penetrating belly wound.

Hence no man could enter the battle and move in the middle unwounded or unhurt by the sharpness of bronze weapons unless led by Pallas Athena, holding his hand and warding off the flights of missiles. Many were the Trojans and Achaeans who on that day lay stretched out dead on their faces beside each other. (iv 539–44)

In the beginning of Book V, Homer includes a sort of catalogue of the slain: Odius, chieftain of the Alizones, slain by Agamemnon with a thrust in the back; Phaestus, from the fertile land of Tarne, killed by Idomeneus with a spear in the shoulder; Scamandrius, the hunter, taught by Artemis – she was no help to him here – who was celebrated for his long shots at game in the mountains, had a spear thrust in the back by Menelaus; Phereclus, the master craftsman who had made the ship Paris sailed in to Sparta, had a spear thrust in the buttocks passing into the bladder by Meriones – he fell with a scream; Pedaeus, illegitimate son of Antenor whose wife brought him up as her own, had a spear in the nape of the neck which cut off his tongue – he bit the bronze – by Meges; and Hypsenor, son of the priest of the river Scamander worshipped by the Trojans, had his arm cut off by Eurypylus.[3]

We hear the sounds of war: helmets and shields ring under the impact of stones or reverberate with deep notes as spears glance off the rims of the shields or the armour; shield clashes against shield and breastplate against breastplate; the dead fall to the ground 'with a thud' (v 617), and the chariot axle groans under a heavy load (v 838–9). We are told things that we can readily believe could only be told by someone who had seen them himself. Alcathous was hit in the chest by a spear. The spear penetrated the breastplate and 'struck him in his heart; and the end of the spear vibrated with the pulse' (xiii 440–1).

In the *Iliad* almost all wounds are fatal but, in reality, the battlefield must have been one horrible cacophony of cries of fear and pain. (Perhaps Homer may have refrained from describing, not the cries of pain, but the brutal reality that the wounded were killed immediately.)[4]

Still, not all wounds are fatal. Aias knocks Hector down with a thrown rock – the heroes fight over the prostrate Hector – and Hector is removed from battle. He vomits blood, but he recovers. Diomedes is wounded by an arrow – fired by Pandarus – which passed through his breastplate into his right shoulder. Athena finds him pulling the strap of his shield away from the wound. Sweat has irritated it and he is tending to it (v 100ff, 793–8). Sarpedon, in a simultaneous exchange of spear casts, kills his opponent but is wounded in the thigh by his enemy's spear, which grazed the bone. His comrades drag him from the field to safety, never thinking to remove the spear so he could walk. He thought that he was going to die, either killed by his wound or by the Greeks pursuing him. Hector protects him and Sarpedon is taken into the shade of an oak tree. His companion removes the spear and Sarpedon faints (v 665ff). Agamemnon, Diomedes, and Odysseus all limp off the battlefield, using their spears as canes (xiv 27–39).

(How realistic is the *Iliad*? Philip, the father of Alexander the Great, had so many injuries that his physician wrote an essay, *On the Wounds of Philip*. Alexander was struck with a battle axe on the top of his helmet, received a sword wound in his thigh and was 'shot by an arrow in the leg below the knee, so that splinters of the larger bone came out'; at other times he was struck in the neck with a stone so severely that his 'eye-sight was clouded', received other 'severe wounds' and was shot with an arrow in the chest. The arrow fastened itself in his ribcage.)[5]

Teucer, the Achaean bowman, aims at Hector, misses and hits Gorgythion, the son of Priam. Homer describes his death with the image of a poppy in full bloom which bends over under the weight of its seeds and the water from a spring rain, so Gorgythion's head drooped on his shoulder (viii 306–8). In contemporary vase paintings the melee is brutal – decapitated bodies, a man with an arrow through his head, the slaying and the slain – but artists after Homer depicted dying warriors more like men falling asleep.

Greeks and Trojans used chariots but, according to Homer, they used them more as transportation to battle or in isolated actions against men on foot. Certainly, in the West in Homer's own time armies of chariots no longer fought each other, although 400 years earlier (in the purported time of the Trojan War) armies from Greece to China had corps of hundreds of chariots manned with drivers and archers who rode around the enemy army, loosed volleys of arrows at them and fought each other, chariot to chariot. In the time of Homer the chariot was still a symbol of the aristocracy, but no Greek state had the resources to field an army of chariots. Nonetheless, contemporary vase paintings depict chariots on the battlefield, and Homer's description of their use would appear to reflect actual practice.[6]

Fighting centres around the heroes, and they are heroic to be sure, but they are not supermen: they can be wounded, they know their limits – even Aias, who is the strongest of them all and the greatest fighter next to Achilles, hesitates and withdraws when the Trojans begin to hem him in (v 621f), and Aeneas pulls back when faced by two heroes (v 571). In the *Iliad* men sweat, grow tired, feel fear and suffer from the pain of wounds: no one is safe (xiii 440). Aias' left shoulder joint ached with the effort of holding his shield steady, he fought for breath, gasping, soaked in sweat and spears rang as they glanced off his helmet (xvi 101–11). The heroes feel the joy of battle (xiii 82) and they know fear, but they are not cowards.[7]

> The cowardly man's skin changes colour,
> now to this and now to that,
> nor can he stand fast nor is his spirit calm,
> but he shifts from one foot to the other continually
> and his heart beats violently in his chest,
> as he thinks about his death, and his teeth chatter . . .

Later (vii 310–end) Homer describes the aftermath of battle. Nestor proposes that they agree to a truce with the Trojans so that each side can collect their dead. Agamemnon agrees because the 'living cannot begrudge the dead proper cremation and burial' (vii 408–10). Burial parties gather wood for the pyre and collect the dead in ox-carts. (As always Homer adds a realistic touch, that the men collecting the dead had to wash the blood off their faces before they could recognise them.) They bring them back to camp, make a pyre and burn them for, otherwise, blowflies and worms would infest the bodies and the bodies would rot. Some men cry. When the pyre has burned down overnight, and after some of the mourners have collected the bones of their comrades to return to their homes, they heap up a barrow over the pyre, and then they feast.

In Book VI Homer does not let us forget that the war is not just about the heroes. A family scene foreshadows the death of Hector, the destruction of Troy, the brutal murder of his baby son and the enslaving of his wife, Andromache. Hector imagines Andromache's fate should the Trojans lose and the Greeks take their city, 'when someone of the bronze-cloaked Achaeans leads you away in tears, taking away from you your day of freedom' (vi 454–5).

He lamented more for her than for his father, mother and brothers, but amid his lament is a light moment – Homer always gives us a moment of humanity (vi 466ff). Hector reached for his child, Astyanax, 'but the child cried out and buried himself in the bosom of his nursemaid, terrified at the sight of his dear father', the glittering bronze and the horsehair crest of the helmet 'and his dear father and beautiful lady mother laughed and Hector removed the helmet from his head' and held his baby son. Andromache gave vent to her fears for him. He stroked her cheek and said (vi 487), 'No man exists who can send me to Hades against my fate'. Who in the *Iliad* is not a victim?

All this – Hector, Andromache, Astyanax, the very walls of Troy – will be swept away as though they never were, these men and their mighty works: the defensive wall and the trench the Greeks made to protect their ships, and the barrow over the dead. Apollo and Poseidon with the help of the rains of Zeus will divert the rivers and flood the plain and sweep the remnants of the destruction out to sea and cover everything with new sand so that not a trace of the Greeks remain. In a generation no visitor will find any sign that a great war was fought here, that men died here and were buried here, or that a great city stood here (xii 1–34).

This, then, is war as Homer conceived it: the arming; the mustering of the eager and the hesitant; the clash; the wounds; the sounds of battle; the individuals killing and being killed; the burial of the dead; and, in the end, although not the end of the *Iliad*, the sack of Troy and the murder or enslavement of the Trojans. And all the horrible carnage of the *Iliad*, remember, is to fulfil Zeus' vow to Thetis to make Agamemnon pay for his treatment of Achilles.

War (that is, Ares) is hated by men and gods (v 31, 455). When Ares is wounded Zeus says to him (v 888–91), 'Don't come sit here and whine to me, you treacherous brat. You are the most hateful to me of all the gods who hold Olympus. Always you love strife and wars and battles.' But peace is found only in a single scene on Achilles' shield, the marvellous shield wrought by the blacksmith of the gods, Hephaestus. On the shield is a city at war and a city at peace (xviii 490–540). In the city at peace young men are dancing in a wedding procession which draws women to the doors of their houses to watch, while other men assemble in the market place to settle a homicide and prevent a blood feud. Neither side is willing to compromise, but the judges speak and the one who speaks the best will receive two bars of gold. The city is not free of violence but, rather, it has developed a procedure to deal with violence to avoid blood feuds.

The shield shows life in all its facets and vigour. It emphasises what Achilles and all the other participants at Troy have to lose because, as Hector says, 'Ares deals death to those who deal death' (xviii 309). (One cannot imagine finding anywhere in the *Iliad* 'The old lie: *Dulce et decorum est / Pro patria mori*'.)

In the world of Homer war permeates everything and involves everyone. A person may be living peacefully in his town one moment and the next be fighting for his own life, and his family, and his property.

The *Iliad* is filled with the tragic loss of sons, fathers, brothers, husbands and of friends, and no friendship is as detailed and stirring as the friendship between Patroclus and Achilles, and no loss is so consequential as the death of Patroclus. The last books of the *Iliad* are dedicated to the story of loss, vengeance and grief.

In Book IX Agamemnon despairs because, without Achilles, the Greeks are in desperate straits. Aias and Odysseus visit Achilles to try to persuade him to help. They find him strumming a lyre and singing songs of heroic deeds while Patroclus, his inseparable companion, sits quietly at his side. In the midst of war Achilles has made his own peace. Achilles and Patroclus rise and greet their visitors. Patroclus fetches more wine and Achilles arranges a feast: they prepare the fire, cut the meat, put it on spits, roast it and then set all before their guests. Patroclus performs the sacrifice and then the four eat and drink. After the meal the envoys try to persuade Achilles to help the Achaeans.

Achilles analyses his choice: he can remain, fight, die young and win everlasting glory, or he can go home, live in peace to a ripe old age and be unknown. However, he does neither. He does not reconcile with Agamemnon and reenter combat, but he does not sail away either. The envoys depart but leave Achilles' old tutor for whom Patroclus prepares a soft bed. Then Achilles and Patroclus retire to their own beds, side by side, each with a woman companion. Homer gives us a sort of army-camp domestic scene.

After this failed attempt at reconciliation, one by one all the heroes are wounded and withdraw from combat, even though Agamemnon for once fights like a hero. In Books XI–XV the Trojans press on the ships. Aias alone is keeping the Trojans from firing the ships . . . and he is exhausted. The Greeks appeal to Patroclus to come in Achilles' armour with the Myrmidons to stop the Trojans.

In Book XVI the first ship catches fire and Patroclus asks Achilles to let him defend the ships. 'Poor Patroclus, not knowing he was pleading for his own doom.' Achilles relents, but orders – indeed, begs – Patroclus not to advance on the Trojans but to defend the ships only. Patroclus is carried away and advances into the plain and there he meets Sarpedon, the son of Zeus. Even Zeus cannot save his son from Fate. He watches Patroclus kill Sarpedon and sends down a shower of blood, foreshadowing the grief of Achilles . . . and also Priam and Thetis and so many more even into our own time.

Patroclus and Hector fight after Apollo encourages Hector. Apollo punches Patroclus in the back, dazing him and knocking his armour off. A Trojan spears him first and Hector finishes him off. With his last words, Patroclus predicts that Achilles will kill Hector. Hector retorts, who knows, Achilles is mortal, too.

In Book XVII the two sides fight over Patroclus and Hector strips him of Achilles' armour. He wants the body, too. Hector is a hero; he is noble, he is fighting for his native city, we admire him – but he is no less brutal than the other heroes. He wants to cut off Patroclus' head and feed the body to the dogs of Troy. The Greeks recover Patroclus' body. Hector puts on Achilles' armour and, in his moment of glory, Zeus pities him because he will never return from the battlefield or to the arms of Andromache.

Hector tries to capture Achilles' horses – they have refused to move, weeping for their lost driver, their manes trailing in the dust – and Zeus protects them.

All this time, while the Greeks pick up the body of Patroclus, Achilles does not know his friend is dead.

In Book XVIII when Achilles learns of the death of Patroclus, he falls into agonising grief; he pours ashes and dirt in his hair, all his women gather around him and wail, he exclaims that life now has no meaning for him, and his mother Thetis comes with her sea nymphs and holds him in her arms, consoling her son.

Achilles' grief cannot be assuaged. He has Patroclus' body cleaned and vows to hold the funeral only after he has brought back Hector's body and twelve living Trojans to sacrifice.

In Book XIX Agamemnon returns Briseis (the girl he took from Achilles); she is consumed with grief for Patroclus and tells her story, how she lost three brothers to the Achaeans and Achilles killed her husband, but Patroclus dried her tears and promised that she would be the wife of Achilles. Each woman, as she wails, grieves for her own wrongs.

In Books XX and XXI Achilles massacres the Trojans. They flee everywhere across the plain and the gates are thrown open to admit them. Only Hector remains outside.

In Book XXII Achilles kills Hector.

The Trojans have all fled within the city but Hector remains outside. His father, Priam,

> shrieked aloud and struck his head with his fists and, filled with piteous fear, he stretched out his hands and called to his son, 'Hector, my dear son, do not wait for that man who is the greatest of all of them [...] he will kill you. Pity your parents. Pity my poor heart and the mother who bore you'. (xxii 38ff)

Hector debates with himself: if he goes inside he will suffer shame because he advised the army to remain outside. Better death than shame and, for that matter, he might defeat Achilles, but then he sees Achilles in the distance and he wonders if he can make a deal.

> But how? I could lay down my mighty shield, perhaps take off my helmet, and lean my spear against the wall. I could offer him Helen and all the precious booty with her, all that Paris loaded into his roomy ship, and to divide the Trojan riches in two and give them half (xxii 110ff).

But then he sees Achilles almost upon him and he trembles, he turns and he flees. Three times they run a circuit, running 'for the life of Hector the horse tamer' (xxii 161). They run as in a dream when one can never catch the one he pursues and the one pursued can never escape. Above them Zeus holds the scales of fate; the scale tips towards Hector's death and Zeus allows Athena to help Achilles. She fools Hector by pretending to be his brother and Hector is ready to fight because it will now be two against one.

Hector tries to make a pact with Achilles, that the victor will return the body of the slain and not mutilate it. Achilles refuses and makes the first spear cast which Hector ducks, taunting Achilles and throwing his own spear which hits the centre of Achilles' shield and glances off. They rush on each other and Achilles stabs Hector in the throat with his spear – a mortal blow – although Hector can still speak and begs Achilles to return his body to his parents. Achilles replies that if he could he would eat Hector raw himself. Every Greek now approaches and stabs Hector with his spear.

Inside the city, Priam laments for his son but no one had brought the news to Hector's wife. She hears the lamentations, runs to the wall and sees his body being dragged back to the Greek ships. She bursts out in a lamentation for herself and for Astyanax, now an orphan to be bullied and pushed aside, to live a miserable existence.

Book XXIII describes the funeral games Achilles organises for Patroclus.

Achilles still rages in his grief for Patroclus; he throws Hector's naked body down in front of the bier, provides a funeral feast for all his Myrmidons, promises to cut the throats of 12 Trojan captives and refuses to wash off the blood of battle until after the funeral of Patroclus. Finally, he falls asleep and the shade of Patroclus appears to him in his dream and asks him to hold the funeral quickly so he can pass over into the realm of the dead and, further, that the two be buried together when Achilles meets his fate. Achilles tries, in vain, to embrace him.

Achilles orders his Myrmidons to gather wood and build the pyre and then he sacrifices horses, dogs and the Trojans, hacking them to pieces. In one of those little details that could convince the reader that Homer was there, Achilles cannot get the pyre to light and he has to pray to the north and west winds to blow and kindle the fire. The pyre burns all night and Achilles pours libations all night long and weeps, and then he gathers the bones and builds a modest barrow which will be completed only when Achilles joins his friend.

Homer then describes the funeral games. The description is full of incidents, but also full of personality and character. The games include a chariot race, boxing, wrestling, a footrace and then a combat between two champions, Aias and Diomedes. The first to draw blood will get the prize, but the crowd becomes afraid for their lives and calls upon them to stop. Finally, there are contests in which the contestants throw a weight of iron, and there is archery and spear-throwing.

The book ends with Achilles doing honour to Agamemnon.

In Book XXIV Achilles tosses and turns, walks beside the ocean and drags Hector's body around the barrow of Patroclus, but nothing soothes his anger and grief. The gods decide to lead Priam into Achilles' tent to beg for the body of Hector. Achilles and Priam weep together for what they have lost and Achilles restrains his anger and shows Priam pity.

Achilles grants Priam eleven days for the funeral and on the twelfth they will fight again. The Trojans have nine days of mourning. Andromache laments for herself, her son, for Hector and for Troy which is now doomed to fall, and Helen laments the 'gentle' Hector who stood up for her and never spoke a harsh word to her. On the tenth day they light the pyre, collect the bones of Hector, put them in a golden chest, put blocks of stone over the chest, and heap up a barrow out in the plain.

The *Iliad* began with the line, 'Tell me, muse, of the wrath of Achilles, son of Peleus', and ends with the line, 'And so they buried Hector, tamer of horses'.

The very style of the *Iliad* reflects the nature of war. Here we learn of the deeds of Diomedes, there of Odysseus, or Aias, or Agamemnon, or Hector. We are taken to one point of combat and then to another, just as today's veteran remembers fighting his own fight, hearing a firefight in the distance, being told of another action somewhere else at the same time, and never knowing the whole story. War is diffuse and the *Iliad* reflects that truth.

Over and over again I, as a veteran, have found myself in the *Iliad*. It portrays war as it is, emotionally and psychologically. When I read that a Greek held a Trojan's head aloft as a trophy (xiv 493–500). I wondered if we no longer took heads as trophies because we were more civilised, or because we didn't have swords to cut heads off. Then a lieutenant in my battalion used his entrenching tool to chop the head off an enemy soldier he had killed. 'Now', he said, 'all I have to do is figure out how to send it home to my wife.'

I found myself entranced by the feel of my rifle, the weight of grenades, the symphony of the PZ: low voices, the distant thunder of the artillery, feet shuffling, packs being settled, rifle magazines being loaded and, in the distance, the beat of the helicopter blades coming closer. No greater excitement exists than combat. For years afterwards I missed it even as I relived it in nightmares.

Unless you are present at the death of a friend, the news of the loss comes slowly; at first you don't believe it and, then, reluctantly, because you have learned the realities of war, you know it to be true. You know heartache as you lie awake and think of your friend, and you cry. You can't eat. You wonder why you have survived. The dead come to you in your dreams and – in my case, anyway – lament that they have lost their lives.

Nestor says, 'Such were my deeds or was it all a dream?' Through the vividness of the experience it stays fresh in the memory and yet with the passage of time it begins to seem remote. (A veteran of the battle of Gettysburg, fifty years later, walked with a Confederate veteran around Culp's Hill where they had both fought. This man – my father knew him – said that it seemed like the battle had happened yesterday ... or never.)

In a combat unit no one wants to associate with someone on whom they cannot depend, someone, for instance, like Paris, who boasts and vaunts and then disappears when the crisis comes. Courage is the fundamental characteristic. Without it, nothing else matters.

All educated Greeks knew the *Iliad* and reacted to it. Thucydides drew upon it as a reliable source for the distant past. The Spartan poet Tyrtaeus used the heroic ideals of the *Iliad* to define citizenship. Alexander the Great modelled himself on Achilles.

When the *Iliad* is translated into film (for instance, *Troy*), and changed for modern audiences, we learn a great deal about ourselves (and, by contrast, about the subtlety and the power of the original). Certainly, in the *Iliad* the Trojan prince Paris has committed a wrong and the Trojans are now suffering, and will suffer, the consequences. Still, Homer does not make the Trojans the bad guys – there are no bad guys in a world in which the gods direct human action – and his balanced account is almost unique in works on war.

We (the modern audience) want Achilles' withdrawal to be for a noble purpose, because Agamemnon and Menelaus are bad men; we want Helen to leave Menelaus not just because she falls for Paris, but because Menelaus is a bad man; we don't want the brave Hector to die or Troy to fall; we want our opponents to be villains; we are not comfortable with the idea, which all veterans come to realise, that the results of combat for the individual are arbitrary and do not confirm moral values.

The *Iliad* remains as vibrant and alive today as it was when it was composed some twenty-eight centuries ago.

CHAPTER II

WAR FROM THE EARLIEST RECORDS TO THE FALL OF THE ROMAN EMPIRE[1]

As far back as we have records – 5,000 years – we have records of war.[2] By the end of the third millennium, the first empire had been established. Armies fought in a phalanx, used onager-pulled carts, had a chain of command and separated units by specialty. Soldiers used the bow, sword, and spear.

Early in the second millennium a people whom we call the Indo-Europeans, living on the steppes of (modern) Russia at the fringes of the civilised world, combined domesticated horses, chariots and the compound bow to create a new weapons system. The chariot-warriors formed an elite warrior class led by a king. They overwhelmed every army they faced: they galloped around the enemy, hit them with arrows – armour was insufficient protection against the compound bow – and, when the enemy formation broke under the onslaught, they pursued the fugitives and annihilated them. The Indo-Europeans (Aryans) conquered India; they entered and occupied the Iranian plateau; they overran Europe (Gauls, Germans, Latins), Greece (Mycenaeans) and Asia Minor (Hittites); they dominated the Silk Route; and they settled on the borders of China (Tocharians). They – or those who adopted the chariot system from them – conquered the Nile Delta (Hyksos) and ruled Egypt for 200 years. All in all, the invention and exploitation of the chariot transformed the world in a way unparalleled until the European marriage of gunpowder and deep-sea ships in the Age of Exploration.

The chariot dominated Eurasia until the beginning of the first millennium when the Persians and the Medes bred a horse which could carry a man on its back. This new warrior – the cavalryman – was more mobile and more stable even in the best of chariot terrain, and could operate in rough country where the chariot could not. The chariot continued to be the symbol of the aristocracy.

By the time the *Iliad* was composed, the centralised society of the Mycenaeans had broken into smaller areas ruled by much-diminished kings. Their armies comprised the well-armed aristocracy and a mass of supporters less well-armed and armoured. Their war was primitive (in the technical sense), although the *Iliad* itself is a sophisticated portrayal of human psychology.

At this time in the Near East, the Assyrian kings were leading their armies in the name of their patron god, Ashur, on rounds of conquest and exploitation. Their armies combined cavalry, infantry, chariots, archers, slingers and engineers. Their formidable siege train could take any city with horrible consequences for the defeated: at best swift decapitation – the heads decorated the king's garden – and, at worst, the slow agony of impalement. At the end of the seventh century, however, internal turmoil encouraged the Chaldaeans of Babylon and the Medes and Persians to invade and conquer Assyria.

The victorious Chaldaeans and Medes divided the Near East between them but, when Cyrus the Great transformed the Median kingdom into the Persian Empire, the Chaldaean king attacked him. Cyrus retaliated and conquered Mesopotamia, then he repelled an invasion by the king of the Lydians (in Anatolia) and conquered Lydia. This conquest brought the Persians into contact with the Greeks of Asia Minor and also the Spartans who had been allies of the Lydian king. Cyrus expanded the Persian Empire to the borders of Egypt, India, and to the eastern shore of the Aegean Sea.

The Persian army was not untypical of the Near Eastern armies that preceded it. Its principle arm was cavalry, furnished by the Persian aristocracy and supported by a mixed force of light infantry and archers. The archers carried light shields, which they would fix into the ground to protect themselves as they knelt and fired their arrows. The infantry, armed with spears and wearing little body protection, would protect the archers if the battle came to hand-to-hand fighting. The army contained engineers and was adept at siege warfare, but it still remained highly mobile.

The Greeks had developed in an entirely different direction, due partly to their mountainous terrain, partly to their politics and partly to their social organisation; they had separated into almost 200 independent city-states (the *polis*). Well-armed and heavily armoured aristocrats would fight the aristocrats of other states in disorganised melees, a sort of duel. The victors of the battle would set the terms of a subsequent peace. The aristocrats fighting in the Lelantine War, the greatest war of the archaic period, agreed not to employ long-range weapons. Their sieges were limited to blockade or surprise attack (like the Trojan War).

The aristocrats who first organised their society into a *polis* gained an enormous advantage over their neighbours. The Argives dominated the northern Peloponnesus and the Spartans conquered their western neighbours, the Messenians, and held the greatest extent of fertile land of any *polis* in Greece. However, in reaction to a Messenian revolt in the seventh century, the Spartans created a system in which every citizen spent his life training for combat as a hoplite in a phalanx.

Hoplites were an innovation of the Argive king, Pheidon, in the middle of the seventh century. He persuaded – or compelled – the newly prosperous, non-aristocratic class to purchase arms and armour – the panoply. The hoplites took their name from their characteristic shield, the *hoplon* – the circular shield (weighing about 15 pounds) which protected the hoplite from chin to knee.[3] They wore greaves, and on their heads the 'Corinthian' helmet, which completely enclosed the head, leaving only a horizontal slit for the eyes and a vertical slit through which to breathe. In the phalanx the hoplites crowded together, shoulder to shoulder, and gained protection from the shield of their neighbour to the right. The phalanx was 8–16 ranks deep and as wide as numbers allowed.

The new hoplite phalanx dominated the battlefield. Within a generation hoplite armies could be found in every *polis*, organised and led by aristocrats but, in many cases, the hoplites were dismissed after the battle with no reward for their service. In some *poleis* the hoplites supported tyrants who ruled outside the law and rewarded their hoplite supporters with grants of land. The hoplites eventually expelled the tyrants and founded 'hoplite democracies' everywhere in Greece.

For the first time in human history armies were formed by, and of, citizens. These citizens, mostly small landholders, trained as much as they could and otherwise led their private lives. The Spartans alone maintained a standing army but, good as it was, and as often as the Spartans won battles, finally they had to accept that they were unable to expand any further by conquest; instead, they created a system of alliances (which we call the Peloponnesian League).

By the beginning of the fifth century Sparta was recognised as a significant power in the eastern Mediterranean, and Athens, now a democracy, as a significant power in Greece. Athens had helped the Ionian Greeks in a failed revolt against the Persian king, Darius, and Darius was determined to punish Athens as part of a greater scheme to conquer the whole of Greece.

In 490 BC the Athenians learned that a Persian fleet had landed on the coast of Attica at Marathon. The Athenians had time to march their phalanx to Marathon, occupy a low range of hills and block the Persian advance. They sent a messenger to ask for help from their allies, the Spartans, and then the Athenians waited. They were reluctant to advance into the plain of Marathon where the Persian cavalry could outflank them, while the Persians, for their part, were reluctant to charge up a slope into a prepared Athenian position. Finally, when the Spartan army was a couple of days' march away, the Persians decided to re-embark and sail elsewhere. The Athenians waited until the horses had been loaded and then they charged through a shower of arrows, closed in hand-to-hand fighting and broke the Persian army. The Persian fleet abandoned the infantry and sailed away. The Athenians killed 6,000 Persians.

Greeks were in no doubt, even after Darius died, that the new Persian king, Xerxes, would return in full force, and most Greeks believed that he would win, so they either remained neutral or sought an accommodation.

However, the Spartans and their allies and the Athenians and their allies were determined to resist. The Spartans had neutralised their immediate rivals in Greece and the Athenians had exploited a new, rich vein of silver to build and man a modern fleet of 200 triremes. Together they formed the League of 'Greeks', which met at Corinth, the sole purpose of which was to fight the Persians, and they agreed that the two Spartan kings would command the fighting forces on land and sea.

The League members decided to use the mountainous terrain to block the Persians by land, while they fought the first battles at sea. Consequently, in 480 BC, the Spartans sent their king Leonidas and an elite force of 300 Spartans to hold the narrow pass at Thermopylae, while the Greek fleet fought a sea battle at Artemisium with the Persian fleet (a combined force of Ionian and Phoenician ships). The battle of Artemisum was a draw, although the Greeks, due to favourable currents, gained possession of all the wrecked ships, destroyed those beyond repair and salvaged the rest. They then decided to withdraw south and prepare to fight again at the island of Salamis.

Leonidas, although he now had no strategic reason to continue to defend Thermopylae, decided to remain, even after he learned that the Persians had found a way around the pass. Perhaps Leonidas stayed to fulfil a Delphic oracle that either a Spartan king would die or Sparta itself would be taken. Leonidas and his men were surrounded and, after a fight in which they broke all their spears, were shot down with arrows.

The Athenian fighting men occupied Salamis, the noncombatants withdrew into the Peloponnesus, and Xerxes occupied Athens. Then the two sides waited. The Greeks did not want to come out into the open sea where the Persians' more manoeuvrable and more numerous ships would have the advantage. Likewise, the Persians did not want to enter the narrows where the Greeks' heavier ships would have the advantage. In this standoff the Athenian commander, Themistocles, sent an envoy to tell the Persian king, Xerxes, that the Greeks were divided in their council – which was true – and that some wanted to withdraw south into the Peloponnesus – also true – and that they were afraid to fight – untrue – and that they were going to withdraw that very night – also untrue. Xerxes believed the story and ordered one-third of the fleet to watch the supposed line of retreat, the other two-thirds to block the main strait and everyone to remain at sea all night.

In the morning the Persians entered the strait but, instead of a demoralised, frightened enemy, they found men ready to fight. As they entered the narrows, the Persian ships ran afoul of each other, they lost their rowing rhythm and the Greeks charged. The Greeks stove in and overturned Persian ships, the Persian crews spilled into the water and the Greeks rowed through the wreckage spearing the helpless oarsmen.

The Persian fleet retreated across the Aegean, Xerxes returned to his kingdom and both sides went into winter quarters. In the spring, the Spartans gathered their allies including the Athenians and marched north to confront the Persians, who were encamped across the Asopus River at Plataea. The Spartan commander, Pausanias, and the Persian commander, Mardonius, both recognised that crossing the Asopus in the face of the enemy would be a tactical error and they held their positions, but the Persian cavalry had its own way in the plain behind the Greek lines – they interdicted supplies and choked off the best source of water.

Pausanias, therefore, decided to make a night withdrawal back across the plain to the foothills, where the army would be protected from cavalry attacks, have ample and accessible water and no problem with supply. Whatever its tactical merits, the actual movement was a mess – the Greek units in the middle, under the impression that the retreat was an admission of defeat, fled in disorder; the Athenians waited for the Spartans to move; and the Spartans, involved in a ferocious argument whether retreat was cowardice, didn't begin their movement until the night was mostly over.

When dawn revealed the abandoned Greek position, Mardonius ordered his army to pursue, unit by unit, as fast as they could. The Persian army caught the Spartans in the open, but the Persians jammed together in the front of the Spartan line, horse and foot mixed, so tightly that they could not manoeuvre. The heavily armoured Spartans fought their way through the lightly armoured Persians to Mardonius, killed him, and broke the Persian force. Meanwhile the Athenians defeated the Thebans, Greek allies of the Persians, and the remnants of the Persian army fled north and were annihilated in Macedonia.

After the victory at Plataea and a subsequent victory at Mycale (in Asia Minor) where the surviving Persian fleet was destroyed, the Spartans withdrew from active participation in the war and the Athenians assumed the leadership of a maritime alliance; the Delian League. In the 50-year period from the Persian campaign to the outbreak of the Peloponnesian War, the Athenians transformed the alliance into an empire for which they offered two justifications: first, simple power politics – they exploited the opportunity they were given; and second, the Greeks now in their empire had been perfectly willing to help the Persians subjugate Athens.

Increasingly during this 50-year period, the Spartans and the Athenians came to consider each other as enemies. The two sides attempted to bring stability to a dangerous situation with a 30-year treaty listing the allies of each side and forbidding either side to attack the other's allies. Nonetheless, the Athenians aided a neutral *polis* in a battle against Corinth, a Spartan ally. After a debate in Sparta, the Spartans decided that the Athenians had broken the treaty. They declared war.

During this 27-year war – the Peloponnesian War (431–404) – the Spartans ravaged Attica in an attempt to goad the Athenians into a set battle, while the Athenian navy raided the Peloponnesian coast. The war revealed the power, and shortcomings, of the Athenian fleet and naval operations in general. The Athenians could raid wherever their fleet could float; they could transport supplies for their operations; they could travel from point to point without having to fight their way through hostile territory; and they could live securely within the walls encircling Athens and its port, because they could supply themselves by sea. On the other hand, fleet operations were far more expensive than they had expected – one siege cost them two-and-a-half-years' income – and knocking an enemy out of the war was much harder than they expected. For the Spartans, once they could not provoke the Athenians into a set battle, they were at a loss for an alternate strategy.

In 430 and 429 the Athenians suffered a devastating plague made worse because all Athenians, except those on campaign, were concentrated in the city – between 25 and 35 per cent of the city population died; nonetheless, the Athenians pressed the war. In 425 they captured some 200 Spartans in a battle on the Messenian coast at Pylos. The Athenians threatened to execute their prisoners if the Spartans invaded Attica; the Spartans, at a loss as to what to do, accepted a plan formulated by the war's one exceptional leader, Brasidas, to send an expedition under his command to northern Greece to liberate the cities subject to the Athenians. Brasidas was so successful – even though he was killed in the fighting – that, in 421, the Athenians agreed to a treaty.

The treaty brought only a brief and troubled interlude (during which the Athenians joined in a battle at Mantinea against the Spartans and were defeated). In 415 the Athenians dispatched a huge fleet to Sicily to conquer Syracuse. The Spartans believed the expedition ultimately was aimed at themselves; they sent an experienced Spartan named Gylippus to direct the defence of Syracuse; in addition, they invaded Attica, built a fort and manned it year-round. In 413 the entire Athenian fleet at Syracuse was trapped and destroyed. Despite this catastrophe the Athenians fought on for 12 years and were defeated in the end by a Spartan subterfuge supported by Persian money and poor Athenian generalship; the Athenian fleet was caught on shore at Aegospotami in the Hellespont and destroyed without a battle.

In the generation from 404–371, the Spartans replaced the Athenians at the head of their empire, defeated their opponents in mainland Greece, occupied the city of their principle enemy Thebes, completely dominated Greece and then lost one battle at Leuctra (371 BC). They saw their homeland of Laconia invaded and devastated, lost Messenia and became a diminished power, squabbling with the Thebans and the Athenians for primacy within Greece, while in the north the Macedonians chose a new king, Philip. (Philip was in his mid-twenties.)

Philip's brother had been killed in a battle against the Illyrians that all but destroyed the Macedonian army and left Philip facing an imminent invasion in which the Illyrians intended to occupy Macedonia while other enemies prepared to join in. Over the winter of 359 Philip reorganised his army: he equipped all soldiers, whether horse or foot, with spears 16–26 feet long (the *sarissa*); he made his cavalry (the Companion Cavalry) more mobile; and he created and trained a 50-man-deep phalanx, which he considered so important that he broke with royal tradition and fought on foot in their ranks. Philip intended that his phalanx would act as an immoveable object on the battlefield against which his cavalry would smash the enemy.

The first test of his new army came in the first winter when Philip surrounded an invading force of Athenians and convinced them to capitulate on the promise of safe conduct out of Macedonia. Philip bribed his neighbours – except the Illyrians – to put off their invasions (with a promise that he would pay them the same each year – a promise he had no intention of keeping) and in the spring he met the Illyrians in battle.

The Illyrians and Macedonians fought to exhaustion – neither side seemed to have an advantage – and Philip asked for a truce to collect his dead. The Illyrians believed, as the convention was, that he was admitting defeat (that he did not have control of the battlefield), and they relaxed. Philip attacked, caught the Illyrians completely by surprise, broke them and sent his cavalry to pursue and kill as many as they could before dark.

Philip's victory established Macedonia as a major power. He campaigned wherever he saw an opportunity, made and broke alliances and used his personal charm, and generosity, to win over adherents in the Greek cities. He bound together in one way or another the centre of the Balkan peninsula, Macedonia, Epirus on the Adriatic coast and Thessaly; he dominated his neighbours, the Illyrians and the Thracians; he drove the Athenians out of their possessions on the coast of Macedonia; and he broke up the Chalcidian League. He was always ready to fight and he had added a siege train to his army – catapults and towers, battering rams, sheds and mural hooks – so that no city was safe; even when he lost an eye in one siege, he persevered until he took the city. Philip was always ready to fight, but he was a superb diplomat and judge of men and he said that he preferred the victories he won through diplomacy, because he did not have to share the credit with his army.

By 340 he had accomplished all his goals except to defeat the Athenians who had persisted in their war against him. He intended to pass through the territory of his ally Thebes and march on the city of Athens. He expected the Thebans to join him or, at worst, to remain neutral, but he had miscalculated. His arch-enemy, the Athenian orator Demosthenes, convinced the Thebans that Philip would attack them too. In the spring of 338 the Athenian and Theban armies met Philip at the battle of Chaeronea. (Alexander, then 18 years old, commanded the Companion Cavalry.)

Philip, opposite the Athenians, allowed the Athenian phalanx to push the Macedonian phalanx back. The Athenians were so excited that they called out that they would push Philip all the way back to Macedonia, but their rapid advance opened up gaps; Philip ordered his phalanx to stop its retreat and push back and, at the same moment, Alexander launched the Companion Cavalry into the gaps. The Athenians, including Demosthenes, broke and ran. Philip turned his phalanx on the Thebans who were caught between Philip and Alexander. As a consequence of his victory, Philip inaugurated a new League of Corinth which included Thebans, Athenians and all the other mainland Greeks (except the Spartans).

In 336 BC Philip was assassinated. Alexander, then 20 years old, was acclaimed king by the Macedonian army. He executed rival claimants and their supporters, sacked Thebes (which had tried to withdraw from the League of Corinth), re-established the Macedonian dominance in the north and then, in 334, crossed into Asia with an army of about 35,000 foot and horse. His stated purpose was to punish Persia for its invasion of Greece, but Alexander's real objective was to conquer and rule the Persian Empire.

Alexander was the best educated and best prepared commander (with the best army) in all of world history. He had been instructed in strategy, tactics, diplomacy and all the requirements of the kingship by a master – his father Philip – and he had been instructed in intellectual matters –

literature (he kept a copy of the *Iliad* under his pillow), history and logic – by the greatest scientific philosopher of the ancient world, Aristotle. Alexander's first objective was to find, fight and kill the Persian king, Darius, in direct combat and thus supplant him as King of the Persians and the Persian Empire. For their part, the Persian nobility intended to fight Alexander as soon as possible and kill him.

Alexander met the Persians soon after he crossed into Asia Minor at the River Granicus. Alexander approached in the late afternoon. His scouts reported the presence of the Persians and that the river was fordable, but had steep banks; Alexander decided to attack immediately and he caught the Persians by surprise. Alexander's advance troops fought their way with difficulty up the riverbank against the massed Persian cavalry and Alexander was soon with them, fighting hand-to-hand. His spear broke. A Persian struck his helmet, lopped off the crest, momentarily stunned him and lifted his arm to strike the fatal blow, but Alexander's bodyguard sheared off the Persian's arm with his sword and the Macedonians drove the Persians from the battlefield. Alexander had struck so quickly that the Persians never brought their sizable force of Greek mercenaries into the battle and Alexander had them surrounded and killed.

Alexander was now able to march, largely unopposed, through the whole of Asia Minor to the city of Issus on the eastern seaboard of the Mediterranean. His successful advance achieved his first objective – to force Darius, in person, to face him in battle – but, as Alexander advanced down the seaboard, Darius got behind him and used the Pinarus River as a defensive bulwark against which Alexander would have to fling his army. As soon as Alexander heard that Darius was behind him he turned, advanced north towards the river and devised his plan on the march.

Alexander's plan in one way was simple – he would charge straight at Darius and kill him – but in the meantime he had to ensure that the rest of his army would not be overwhelmed by the mass of Persians. He identified his left flank as the critical point of the coming battle and he ordered Parmenion, in command of the phalanx, not to lose contact with the shore no matter what happened and then he further reinforced him with cavalry.

In the battle he rode straight at Darius. Darius fled, abandoning his army, his treasure train (enough to pay for all the rest of Alexander's campaigns), and his wife, son, mother and harem.

Subsequently, Darius made an offer to Alexander to cede Asia Minor. Parmenion advised Alexander, 'If I were Alexander, I would accept it', to which Alexander replied, 'So would I, if I were Parmenion'.[4] Alexander's response to Darius was that he, Alexander, was now king of Persia and Darius should approach him as any subject approaches his king. Darius, of course, refused, and prepared to meet Alexander in the heart of the empire. Alexander, meanwhile, advanced down the coast and lay siege to the city of Tyre – its location on an island convinced its inhabitants that it was impregnable. Alexander build a half-mile-long causeway from the main-land to Tyre and advanced siege engines and towers along the causeway and also by sea (on ships lashed together), as the besieged employed every device that the ingenuity of man could devise for the destruction of his fellow man. Alexander drove the siege for seven months, before he took the city and killed, or enslaved, everyone in it.

After Tyre, and with minimal resistance, Alexander entered Egypt. There, Alexander allowed his army the better part of a year to rest, re-cuperate and prepare for the next campaign while he organised Egypt, visited the oracle of Zeus Ammon at the oasis of Siwa (where the high priest greeted him with the word *paidios* – to the priest 'son', but to a Greek ear, 'son of Zeus'),[5] and laid out the future city of Alexandria, which became the seat of the Ptolemies and one of the great cities of the ancient world.

Then Alexander set out to meet Darius. On 1 October 331 BC, he fought Darius at the battle of Gaugamela. Darius intended to use his huge advantage in cavalry to outflank, envelop and overwhelm Alexander's smaller army. In response, Alexander placed a force behind the main body to defend the rear, he refused his flanks so that the enemy cavalry would be driven past his formation and then, all preparations made, he advanced obliquely on the battlefield to outflank the Persian army and disrupt Darius' careful preparations.

Darius' army developed gaps as it tried to move with Alexander, and

Alexander launched his attack into the gaps directly at Darius. Darius fled and Alexander pursued. Alexander took Babylon, fought his way through the Persian Gates into Persia itself, and occupied Persepolis. There he declared the war of revenge was over, he released all the allies who did not want to enlist in his army as mercenaries and then, after a pause to let his troops recover from this campaign, he began the final pursuit of Darius. He caught up with him – Darius was dying, stabbed by an usurper – and he continued the pursuit until he caught and punished the murderer. He advanced into the eastern part of the empire and into Bactria (where he won the loyalty of the Bactrians by marrying a Bactrian princess, Roxane). By 327 BC he had established his rule over the whole of the Persian Empire.

From Bactria he entered India and fought the last of his four great battles; the battle of the Hydaspes River (326 BC) against the Indian king Porus. Alexander had to cross a river too deep to ford, do it in the face of an enemy army and fight elephants which terrified his horses. He used a ruse to cross the river and then directed a battle plan in which his cavalry attacked the flanks and avoided the elephants, his phalanx forced them back on their own army, and his combined force gradually squeezed the army of Porus in upon itself until it broke. He captured Porus and asked him how he expected to be treated, Porus replied, 'Like a king', and Alexander reinstated him.[6]

Here, at last, in India, Alexander had to accept the truth that his army would advance no further and he returned to Babylon after suffering an almost fatal chest wound and marching his army across the Gedrosian Desert, the most inhospitable desert in the world. In Babylon, Alexander continued his plans to bring Persians into his army and civil service, but in 323 he fell ill and died.

An army council declared his posthumous son king (Alexander IV), and ruled in his name, but the council split and its members, known as the Successors, fought each other first for control of the united empire and then to establish themselves in independent kingdoms. When the fighting was finally done, Alexander IV was dead – murdered; Ptolemy held Egypt; Seleucus, another of Alexander's boyhood friends, held the Asian Empire (the Seleucid Empire); and the descendants of Antigonus the 'One-Eyed' (one of Philip's generals) held Macedonia.

In 280 BC Pyrrhus, the king of Epirus (and one of the Successor's 'Successors'), accepted an invitation to come to Italy to protect Tarentum from the Romans. As commander of a veteran army comprising phalanx, cavalry and war elephants, Pyrrhus anticipated that the task of defending Tarentum from an Italic (and barbarian) people would not be difficult, but from his first exclamation when he saw the Romans pitching camp – 'These people are not barbarians!' – to his remark after a hard-fought victory – 'One more such and we are lost!' – Pyrrhus learned that he was facing a new and different kind of force in the Mediterranean world. Tactically his 'Alexandrian' army was more than a match for the Roman legionary army, but the Romans were his superior in organisation, tenacity and strategy. In the end, although the Romans never won a battle, they forced Pyrrhus to abandon Italy.

With their victory over Pyrrhus and the capitulation of Tarentum, the Romans completed the unification of Italy. Just a little more than a century before, in 387 BC, the Roman army, a phalanx, had suffered a catastrophic defeat at the battle of the Allia, and the victorious Gauls had occupied Rome and held it for ransom. After the Romans paid, they appointed (according to later tradition) a dictator, Camillus, to reform the army. He expanded the draft to include all citizens with property and he organised them in maniples (comprising two centuries) to give the legion more flexibility. Hence, his army is called the *manipular* army.

Camillus created a new tactical formation, splitting the army on the battlefield into a leading formation – the *hastati* – and then, after a gap, a second formation – the *principes* – and then, after a wider gap, three more formations in his army, but in the later army one more – the *triarii*. In theory, and often enough in practice, the manipular army's first formation, the *hastati*, could receive an all-out charge, fight the attackers, tire them, wound and kill some of them and give way to the fresh second formation, the *principes*, who would defeat the attacking force or, at worst, attrite them more, so that the third formation, the *triarii*, would defeat them. The

Camillan army underwent many reforms during the course of Roman history, but its basic conception remained the same until the third century AD.

Just as the Greeks had gone through a social struggle between the aristocracy and the hoplite class so, too, the Romans had to settle a dispute between the patricians (aristocrats) and the plebs (the common people), who were now expected to fight in the ranks. In the end, the plebeians won equal political rights including the right to hold the highest office, the consulate. The Romans proved the efficacy of the reforms a generation later when they checked the Gauls in a battle at the Anio River and, subsequently, in a series of wars, compelled their northern neighbours, the Etruscans, and their immediate neighbours, the Latins, to accept their leadership; they expanded their control across central Italy and finally to the south in four wars against a mountain people, the Samnites. They built a network of roads and colonies throughout Italy and they forced the Gauls to settle north of the Po River. (Without the Romans, the Gauls would have occupied the whole of Italy.)

Thus, by 275, the Romans had established a new political system in Italy: they granted some Italians Roman citizenship, others the status of federated allies, and bound the rest by treaty. The Romans thus created an enormous pool of citizens and as many more Latins and allies to call upon for military service. Their system – based on their understanding that citizenship was a collection of rights and duties, not a question of birth – was unique in the western world. Their defeat of Pyrrhus caught the attention of King Ptolemy, who asked the Alexandrian scholars to place the Romans properly in a Greek context. The scholars concluded that the Romans were, in reality, an amalgamation of native Italic peoples and refugees from Troy. The king, through luck or foresight, made an alliance with the Romans; this alliance preserved the Ptolemies' rule for two-and-a-half centuries.

The only other comparable power in the central Mediterranean was Carthage. Carthage was a powerful city-state which controlled a significant hinterland and a nexus of forts and trading stations throughout the western Mediterranean. For centuries, Carthaginians had fought Greeks for control of Sicily, with first one and then the other gaining the upper hand, but neither able to drive the other from the island. Carthage had sent a garrison to the city of Messana (in the northeast corner of Sicily) at the request of an Italic mercenary force, the Mamertines, who had seized the city, expelled the men, co-opted their wives and families and then asked the Carthaginians for help. The Mamertines soon regretted that decision and, in 264, they appealed to the Romans, as fellow Italians, to help expel the Carthaginian garrison and defend them against the Messanan men and the Syracusans and their tyrant, Hiero.

The Roman people voted to intercede in what developed into the First Punic War (264–241). A consul (nicknamed The Log) crossed the straits of Messana with a small army. The Carthaginian commander thought he had no choice but to withdraw. (He was executed for this mistake in judgement.) The Roman consul then fended off a combined Carthaginian and Syracusan force and drove the Syracusans back to Syracuse. The next year the Romans convinced the Syracusan tyrant, Hiero, to desert the Carthaginians, to pay the Romans an indemnity and to become an ally. In return, the Romans called Hiero 'king'. He remained a faithful ally until his death.

The Roman strategy is simply stated – occupy the Carthaginians on land in Sicily, gain supremacy at sea and send an expedition to Africa to attack Carthage. In the first phase of their strategy the Romans, after vicious fighting and strained supplies, seized Agrigentum, the Carthaginians' main supply depot on the southern coast of Sicily. (Their thorough, systematic and complete plundering of Agrigentum shocked the Sicilian Greeks.) The Romans realised that they could win this war only if they developed a navy of their own but, furthermore, that they could defeat the experienced Carthaginian fleet only if they developed innovative tactics at sea. They built a fleet of the most modern fighting ship, the quinquereme, and they invented a boarding device, the crow, a hinged plank with a spike at the end which linked Roman and Carthaginian ships together, so that Roman soldiers could cross to the Carthaginian ship and slaughter the crew. The Romans never lost a battle at sea.

By 256 BC the Romans had confined the Carthaginians to the western end of Sicily, invaded Africa, defeated the Carthaginian army there, detached the peoples of the Carthaginian hinterland and seemed to be one victory away from complete success. However, the Carthaginians hired a Spartan mercenary, Xanthippus, who reorganised the Carthaginian army and defeated the Romans. The Romans had to withdraw from Africa, they lost their fleet to a storm and they decided to concentrate totally on operations in western Sicily, but they could not dislodge the brilliant Carthaginian commander, Hamilcar Barca. Finally, in 242, the Romans made one last supreme effort: they raised money from individual Senators, rebuilt their fleet, defeated the Carthaginians at the Aegates Islands and forced them to come to terms, to pay the Romans a cash indemnity and cede the island of Sicily (the first Roman province).

Between 241 and 218 the Romans created a defensive zone around Italy – they occupied Sardinia and Corsica, eliminated the Illyrian pirates in the Adriatic and defeated the Gauls north of the Po River. With a manpower reserve for the legions of 500,000 men they seemed completely secure, and they would have been if it had not been for the Carthaginian commander in Spain, the son of Hamilcar Barca: Hannibal.

The Romans anticipated war: in 218 they sent one consul with his army south to cross into Sicily and from there to invade Africa while the other consul and his army sailed west to fight Hannibal in Spain, but Hannibal stole a march on the Romans. He crossed the Alps, entered northern Italy and launched the Second Punic War (218–201). The consul in the south marched north with his legions to hold the line of the Po River, but Hannibal eluded him, crossed the Po and took advantage of the consul's aggressiveness to lure him through an icy river, the Trebia, onto a field already prepared with an ambush. Hannibal's men were rested, fed and warm, and he had elephants (which proved to be ineffective against the Roman legions but scattered their Gallic allies). He attempted to envelop the Romans – his army killed many Roman soldiers – but the core of the Roman army broke through his battle line and fled to nearby towns. The Battle of the Trebia was the first of Hannibal's three great victories in Italy and proved his dictum, 'The Romans do not know how to fight this kind of war'.[7]

The Roman commander blamed the weather. The Romans, still confident, prepared to prevent Hannibal from breaking into central Italy. The two consuls, each with an army, blocked the two more likely approaches and a *praetor* guarded the third. Hannibal again moved before they expected, by a route they thought impassable, and out-marched them. One consul pursued him while the other converged. Their plan was to catch Hannibal between the two Roman armies, but Hannibal struck first. He set an ambush at night at Lake Trasimene; in the early morning the consul marched into the kill zone and Hannibal's army annihilated him and his legions (the only case in military history of one army successfully ambushing another). By this victory Hannibal opened the whole of Italy to his advance and forced the Romans to admit that they had been defeated in a major battle.

In this emergency they chose a dictator, Fabius, who tried to limit the damage Hannibal could do by following him, cutting off stragglers and limiting his ability to plunder. He believed that Hannibal was unique, that the Romans were totally unprepared to fight him, and that they should avoid battle with him at all costs. The dictator was criticised for his tactics and given the derisive nickname 'Delayer'. Subsequent events proved the wisdom of his strategy and earned him a line in an epic poem – 'One man by delaying saved the state.'[8]

In 216, when Fabius' term as dictator was over, the Romans sent both consuls with a combined army against Hannibal. At Cannae the Roman army was surrounded and annihilated in the greatest catastrophe the Romans had experienced since the Gauls occupied their city. Cannae was the culminating defeat of three battles in which the Romans lost close to 100,000 men. Many Italian cities and peoples now joined Hannibal: Gauls destroyed a Roman army in the north; the Carthaginians in Spain defeated the Roman army, inflicted heavy casualties and killed the commanders; the city of Capua, whose citizens the Romans considered to be Roman, welcomed Hannibal; Syracuse broke with the Romans; and Philip, the king of Macedonia, made an alliance with Hannibal. Nonetheless, the core of Italy remained loyal, Ptolemy sent aid from Egypt and, as the Greek historian,

Polybius, wrote, 'The Romans are never so much to be feared as when they themselves have the most to fear'.[9]

The Romans used their tremendous organisational abilities to build up the number of legions in the field. They assigned one army to follow Hannibal, another to besiege Syracuse, another to besiege Capua, another to go to Spain, another to operate in northern Italy, another to guard the city of Rome and a fleet to watch events in Greece and raise opposition to Philip. By the end of the war the Romans had 26 citizen legions (and as many more composed of Latins).

Publius Cornelius Scipio, the son of the Roman consul killed in Spain, was chosen by the popular assembly to succeed his father; he had to be given a special grant of *imperium* (the power to command troops) because he had never been consul or *praetor*. When he arrived in Spain, he infused the survivors with a new spirit and surprised and captured the enemy depot at New Carthage. He reequipped the army with the Spanish sword and he retrained the three formations of the army (the hastati, the principes and the triarii) to act as independent units so that the Roman army could move in any direction and each formation could split, move laterally and outflank an enemy army. With his new army he defeated the Carthaginians in two battles and expelled them from Spain.

One of the defeated armies, led by Hasdrubal (the brother of Hannibal), crossed the Alps to join Hannibal, but the Romans cornered Hasdrubal in northern Italy, defeated him, killed him and threw his severed head into Hannibal's camp. Scipio returned to Italy a hero; he was elected consul and, in 204, he led an invasion of Africa, defeated the Carthaginians in three battles and forced them to recall Hannibal. Scipio and Hannibal met at the battle of Zama. Hannibal, outnumbered in both cavalry and infantry, organised his army, as only he could, to gain every tactical advantage but, just the same, the Roman army – and Scipio – was more than a match for him; the Romans killed or captured almost the entire Carthaginian army and thus won the Second Punic War.

Rome had become the most powerful state in the Mediterranean. In a series of wars over the next half-century they defeated the Macedonians twice and divided Macedonia into four states; defeated the Greeks and razed Corinth; defeated the Seleucid Empire and reorganised the political boundaries of the eastern Mediterranean; annihilated or expelled all Gauls from Italy north of the Po; and razed Carthage. In Spain, they pursued a policy of colonisation and control which devolved into two centuries of the most brutal warfare before, as one of their enemies said, 'They make a desert and call it peace'.[10]

The conquests put an enormous strain on the Roman republic. Roman nobles could make fortunes if they gained command of an army. In the field they were completely free to act as they pleased and keep all the proceeds of pillage. As a system to expand and conquer it worked very well because the military operations paid for themselves, but the continuous service without any pension system impoverished the citizen-soldiers. In 133 and 123 two brothers, Tiberius and Gaius Gracchus, attempted to create a system to provide land to the poor and, in particular, to veterans. The attempts led to riots and bloodshed inside Rome without stabilising the Roman army.

At the end of the second century, a minor war in Africa led to a revolution in the recruitment of the Roman army. The war was prolonged, the Roman soldiers were unwilling and the popular assembly was dissatisfied with the conventional leadership of the nobles. Marius, the first man in his family to be consul, was elected on the promise that he would not draft more soldiers for the campaign in Africa. He kept his word by throwing recruitment open to Roman citizens who had no property. He reorganised the army so that: all soldiers were uniformly equipped; the cohort (three maniples) became the smallest tactical unit; the distinctions in equipment and status between hastati, principes and triarii were eliminated; each soldier received a pilum; and the light-armed troops became a separate unit (not attached to the hastati). Marius' reforms created a professional army and fundamentally altered the balance of political power in the later Roman republic – many Romans now made their living solely from military service and their loyalty was given only to their commander.

Marius won the war in Africa just in time to confront a far greater foe:

two German tribes had annihilated a double-consular army in southern Gaul. One tribe was crossing the Alps into northern Italy while the other was advancing through Gaul towards Italy. The Roman army facing the first tribe took one look at the ferocious Germans tobogganing down the slopes of the mountains on their shields and ran, but Marius' soldiers were completely confident in him and in themselves and they were ready to fight. They annihilated the German tribe in Gaul and then, joining the Roman army in Italy, annihilated the other tribe.

The Romans were supreme everywhere, except in Italy. The Latins, who were doing more than their share of the fighting without recompense, now demanded citizenship and a share in the benefits accruing from the conquests. When their demands were rejected, they rebelled. The Romans suddenly found themselves facing an army every bit as good as their own, organised exactly the same, as experienced as theirs and equally well led. Roman losses were so severe, and so heart-wrenching, that they decided henceforward to bury their dead in the field. Nonetheless, the Romans managed to survive the first year of war and then broke the rebellion by offering amnesty and citizenship to any Italian who came over, in person or city by city. In the end, the Romans extended citizenship to all the free inhabitants of Italy.

However, a personal rivalry between the aged Marius and the new-comer Sulla led to a civil war, which Sulla won; the civil war tempted some eastern powers to declare themselves free of Rome but Sulla's successors – Pompey, Crassus, and Caesar – reintegrated the east into the empire, put down piracy throughout the Mediterranean and suppressed a slave revolt in Italy (Spartacus). Pompey, Crassus and Caesar made a secret pact – the triumvirate – to direct the politics of Rome. Under the influence of the triumvirate Caesar was given the command of Transalpine Gaul and Crassus was given the command against the Parthians in the east.

Caesar entered 'long-haired' Gaul in response to a provocation by the Helvetian Gauls; he pursued the Helvetians, fought them and defeated them. Thereafter, he responded to a request by his Gallic allies to drive the Germans from Gaul, he defeated the German king and he forced the surviving Germans to flee across the Rhine. At this point, he established his troops in winter quarters inside Gaul and the next year began a systematic conquest. He isolated Gaul by crossing the Rhine and harassing the Germans. (He built a bridge across the Rhine in ten days, a notable engineering feat which American engineers in World War II were determined to beat.) Caesar also crossed to Britain twice and compelled the British tribes to agree to terms.

Through the first years of his conquest, Caesar could always count on some Gauls to help him subdue other Gauls but, in the end, the Gauls united under one commander, Vercingetorix. Caesar cornered Vercingetorix in the city of Alesia (which was located on a commanding height) and encircled Alesia with a double wall. He defended the walls against attacks from within and without, led a detachment of troops in person and, in a very close affair, defeated the last hope of the Gauls to breach the walls, defeat him and remain free. After Caesar's conquest, Gaul became one of the richest and most vital parts of the Roman Empire.

Caesar was not an innovator. He made no significant changes in the legionary army. He was no greater strategist than other Roman commanders and, if we had the commentaries of Scipio, Sulla or even Trajan, we might revise his place in the canon of great commanders but, all that being said, he was the complete master of his army's capabilities and he used them to their maximum effect. In addition, his *Commentaries* are considered one of the greatest works of Latin prose and they have influenced generals ever since.

His fellow triumvir, Crassus, was not so successful. He invaded the Parthian Empire with inadequate preparations and was cut off and surrounded by a superior force of cavalry which overwhelmed the Roman cavalry and showered the infantry with arrows. Crassus surrendered and was beheaded: his head was displayed to the Parthian king as a prop in a play written by Euripides (the *Bacchae*).

The two surviving triumvirs, Caesar and Pompey, fought a civil war from one end of the Mediterranean to the other which concluded with Pompey's head being presented to Caesar and Caesar triumphant everywhere. Caesar, however, had not figured out how to rule a state that still clung to republican ideals in circumstances that no longer supported a republic; he was suspected of plotting to become king and he was assassinated on the Ides of March, 44 BC.

Marc Antony, Caesar's heir Octavian and the assassins all contended for supremacy in Rome, but Octavian outmanoeuvred them. With the help of the Senate he forced Antony to agree to his terms; with the help of Antony, he eliminated the assassins; and, with the deft use of propaganda – that Antony was doing the bidding of an Egyptian woman, Cleopatra – he turned Antony's own troops against him and became the sole master of the Roman world.

He learned from the mistakes of Caesar – he rejected permanent office and reserved only two powers for himself; first, the *tribunician power* which gave him the right to address the Senate, to have personal protection, and to veto all business; and second, the *greater imperium* which gave him command over all the armies of Rome. He preserved all Roman institutions in form, so that he could claim that he had restored the Republic, even though he allowed no significant business to be transacted, nor any individual to hold office, without his approval. He was granted the title 'father of his country' and the name Augustus.

The tribunician power and the greater imperium became the defining powers of the emperors. The greater imperium allowed Augustus to replace a system of multiple commanders vying for wealth and power with one commander and one central direction. When that commander was competent the system worked; imperial income matched expenses, the empire was stable and the borders were secure. When the commander – the emperor – was incompetent, the whole empire was at risk.

The first challenge to the imperial system came when Augustus died and the Senate was faced with the question of the succession. After some hesitation the Senate accepted that Tiberius, the adopted son of Augustus, would continue to hold the imperial powers and be, in effect, emperor. The issue of the succession continued to trouble the empire, but that first succession settled one question – there would always be an emperor. The descendants of Augustus and Tiberius, the Julio-Claudians, ruled Rome until the overthrow of Nero in AD 68 and the assumption of power by a new family, the Flavians, in AD 69. The Flavians ruled until the end of the first century.

In the first century the emperors subdued the greater part of Britain but their attempt to conquer Germany failed and they accepted the Rhine and the Danube Rivers as the natural boundary between Germans and Romans. They created an imperial bureaucracy and extended Roman citizenship outside Italy to prominent individuals and occasionally through a block grant to cities. They established the absolute power of the emperor and the diminished role of the Senate. By the end of the first century, the emperors were being addressed as 'master and god'. Although most of the emperors followed a policy of conciliation with the Senate, the basic ruling philosophy of the emperors could be summed up in one imperial statement: 'Let them hate so long as they fear'.[11]

They established a professional army of approximately 26 titled legions (for example, *Legio VI Ferrata* 'Iron', *Legio VIII Augusta*) and assigned the legions to semi-permanent posts. They established standard terms of service – 20 years for citizens and longer for foreigners – and retirement benefits: land for citizens, citizenship for foreigners. The emperors also kept a personal guard, the Praetorian Guard, which served a shorter term, was paid more and performed ceremonial functions.

When Domitian, the last of the Flavians, was murdered without heirs in AD 96, the Senate selected an emperor from their own ranks, an elderly senator named Nerva. He adopted Trajan, the commander of the Roman troops on the Danube and, after Nerva's death in AD 98, Trajan succeeded peacefully. His first challenge was Dacia (modern Romania). The Dacian king had raided the Roman province across the Danube with impunity during the reign of Domitian; he concluded that the Roman Empire had become weak and vulnerable and he continued his raids after the death of Domitian and Nerva. Trajan collected his army, crossed the Danube on a bridge constructed by his engineers, and invaded Dacia.

The first battle was so fierce that Trajan had to tear up his own garments to make bandages for his soldiers, but he won, and he ordered an advance in three columns into the heart of Dacia, converging on the capital and forcing the Dacian king to capitulate. As was Roman practice, the emperor left the Dacian king on his throne as a vassal, but the king concluded that the war had been so costly and so demanding that the Romans would never undertake such a campaign again, and he rebelled. Trajan returned, conducted another arduous campaign, and this time made Dacia a Roman province and resettled it with Roman colonists.

Trajan's final campaign was against Parthia. He won control of Mesopotamia and he intended to make it a province but died in the field and his adopted successor, Hadrian, withdrew. Hadrian – and *his* adopted successor, Antoninus Pius – enjoyed a legacy of peace based on the supremacy of the Roman army and the aggressive campaigns of Trajan. Hadrian delimited the empire with a series of fortifications along the border, the most famous of which is, of course, Hadrian's Wall in Britain. Hadrian travelled to every province of the empire to promote integration and unity through loyalty expressed by emperor-worship. His reign and his successor's reign were, for the most part, peaceful, but Antoninus Pius' adopted successor, Marcus Aurelius, inherited a world which had forgotten the quality of the Roman army and knew only that immense riches lay within reach. In AD 167, Germanic tribes invaded the empire and even entered Italy, while in the east the Parthians tested Roman defences.

Marcus Aurelius sent his co-emperor, Lucius Verus, to conduct the campaign against the Parthians. Verus occupied Mesopotamia, invaded Media and seemed on the verge of incorporating the old empire of Alexander into the new Roman Empire, but his campaign was cut short by a disastrous plague. He died, his army was decimated and the survivors brought the plague back into the empire where it ravaged the civilian population. Marcus Aurelius had to sell his personal possessions and enlist slaves to raise enough troops for his campaign against the Germans.

He was determined this time, once and for all, to solve the German problem, which had vexed the empire since the days of Augustus, by converting Germany into a province. He was successful on the battlefield, but he was forced to suspend the campaign to put down a rebellion in the east and then, when he resumed the campaign and needed perhaps one more year to achieve his objective, he died (in AD 180) and his son,

Commodus, became emperor (ending the age of the 'five good emperors'). Commodus frittered away the accomplishments of his predecessors and he died without a designated heir.

In the inevitable civil war the eventual victor was Septimius Severus. He restored stability to the empire and its borders, but he did so by ensuring the primacy of the army: he increased soldiers' pay; he recruited retired legionnaires into the bureaucracy of Rome and granted equestrian status to centurions; he maintained a single large army under his own personal command; and he divided the rest among smaller command areas so that no commander would be able to challenge him.

After Severus put down his rivals he restored Roman prestige with successful campaigns in Mesopotamia, North Africa and Britain beyond Hadrian's Wall, where he died in 211. His last words were an appeal to his sons, Caracalla and Geta, to keep the army happy and to work together. Caracalla murdered Geta and became sole emperor. In 212 he granted Roman citizenship to all free inhabitants of the Roman Empire. He planned to follow his father's successes in Mesopotamia by conquering Persia, but his praetorian prefect accidentally learned that he was marked for execution and he struck first.

In the following half-century of civil war and foreign invasion the empire fragmented and was almost overwhelmed. The Roman army proved superior to its enemies, but with so many fronts and so many rival claimants to the throne, the army was unable to meet every threat. Then, beginning in AD 268, a series of emperors from Illyria (the 'soldier emperors', 268–85) defeated the Germanic invaders, checked the expansion of Persia, defeated the independent state of Palmyra and reunited the empire.

In 285 the new emperor, Diocletian, initiated a series of reforms. He systemised the succession and the military so it could protect the empire's borders. He divided the empire into two halves, each ruled by its own emperor, the 'Augustus', and two 'Caesars', the designated successors. Each of the four had his own court and his own army and the Augusti assigned areas of operations to their Caesars. Diocletian designed the system to avoid civil war and to concentrate forces where they were most needed while offering flexibility and mutual support through the four separate armies. He secured the frontier by dividing the frontier troops into many small units, each with permanent responsibility for a section of the border, and he emphasised speed of movement by increasing the role of the cavalry in the main army. Diocletian also reformed the imperial bureaucracy so that it would be staffed entirely by veterans and he created a chain of command which reached down to every inhabitant of the empire. This system, the tetrarchy, brought stability to the empire, repopulated the areas of the borderlands which had been devastated by invaders and established peace and security, so long as Diocletian remained emperor.

When Diocletian retired in 305, the designated successors and the sons of the emperors began a civil war which lasted for 20 years until, ultimately, Constantine defeated the last of his western rivals at the battle of the Milvian Gate, where he had a vision of the Chi Rho and heard a voice proclaim, 'In this sign you will conquer'.[12] He attributed his victory, and his subsequent victories which enabled him to become the sole emperor of the united empire, to Christ, he adopted Christianity as his personal religion and, without actively persecuting pagans, he nonetheless ensured that the empire would be Christian.

As sole emperor he faced a formidable task. He had to defend the borders of the empire with one army instead of the tetrarchy's four. Consequently, he again increased the size of the cavalry, enlisting bands of German mercenary cavalry and reducing the size of the legion to 1,000 men, rearming them with spears and round shields – they fought as a closed phalanx. He intended that the forts along the frontier would stop minor incursions, sound the alarm if faced with a large force of invaders, impede its advance and become the centre of defence when the regular army arrived.

Constantine was unable to solve the real weakness of the empire: the imperial apparatus, including the army, required more money than the empire could afford and he was forced to order ever more severe tactics to raise money, even as he tried to control the expense of maintaining a professional army – pay for 20 years of service and then pensions – by hiring mercenaries for a single campaign. He rejected a proposal to draft Roman citizens for a two- or three-year enlistment because, when their enlistment was up and they returned home, they might support a local rebellion. Constantine successfully protected the borders of the empire until his death in 337, but in the civil war following his death Germans invaded Gaul and the Persian Empire declared war.

Julian, a collateral relative of Constantine, successfully defended Gaul and concluded a generation of civil war in 361. He incorporated German units into his army and considered them so important that he learned to speak German. He rejected Christianity and promoted paganism, but he was killed in 363 while fighting the Persians in Mesopotamia. Julian's immediate successors, two brothers who were Christians, divided the empire between them, as Diocletian had, each with his own court; they secured the borders again, minimised, though they did not eliminate, the Persian threat and established a secure succession. All subsequent emperors were Christian and they outlawed pagan practices one by one including, finally, the Olympic games.

Then, seemingly out of the blue, a new and terrifying force threw Europe into turmoil. The Huns, a nomadic horse people – they introduced the stirrup into Europe – had migrated from the borders of China. They wiped out the East Goths and so terrified the West Goths that they begged the Romans to admit them into the empire. The Romans agreed, let the Goths cross the Danube and then treated them so shabbily that the Goths marched on Adrianople in 378, massacred the imperial army and killed the emperor of the East. The emperor of the West appointed Theodosius to take his place and restore the situation. Theodosius conciliated the Goths, used them to defend the line of the Danube and recruited them to form a new army consisting of Romans and Germans in equal proportion. Theodosius succeeded in reuniting the empire, but upon his death in 395 his two sons divided the empire between them.

Theodosius had preserved the empire, but he had allowed a Gothic tribe to remain within the borders of the Roman Empire as a federated, and semi-independent, people. Although he had been able to control them, his son could not, and in 410 Alaric, king of the Goths, sacked Rome. German tribes crossed the Danube and the Rhine and resettled the western empire; the eastern empire survived the onslaught and gradually evolved into the Byzantine Empire. The emperors also depended on large numbers of foreign mercenaries formed by national groups and they had to contend with a new challenge. Attila, the king of the Huns, created a Hunnic Empire centred in modern Hungary, which threatened the Roman Empire east and west. In 451, however, Attila's attempt to conquer Gaul failed when a coalition of Alans, Germans and Romans defeated him at the battle of Chalons. He died soon after and his empire disintegrated. The last Roman emperor in the west was deposed in 476.

CHAPTER III

WAR FROM THE FALL OF THE ROMAN EMPIRE TO OUR OWN TIMES[1]

In the West, the triumph of the Germanic kingdoms over the Roman imperial army meant also the destruction of the imperial bureaucracy with its taxing authority, discipline and organisation. The Germanic kingdoms wasted their resources in fighting each other; they were unprepared for the challenge presented by the religious revolution of Muhammad at the beginning of the seventh century and they – and the Byzantines – were unable to resist the onslaught of Islam; by the beginning of the eighth century they had lost all of North Africa and Spain and were under threat in 'France'.

In 733, however, Charles Martel (the 'Hammer') defeated the Muslim army at Tours and established the Pyrenees as the border between the Christian and Muslim worlds. His grandson, Charlemagne (742–814), extended his empire to the Elbe including modern France, the Low Countries, Germany west of the Elbe including Bavaria, northern Italy, Switzerland and Austria. In 800, under the auspices of the Pope and the Catholic church, he took the title 'Roman Emperor'. He thus received legitimacy from the church, which provided a measure of organisation throughout Europe (except Spain). Three decades after his death, his kingdom fragmented. Charlemagne's grandson established, or perfected, the feudal system, under which a man would be assigned land by his patron and in return would owe his patron military service; once a year, he was required to show up on horseback at a central meeting place to confirm his continued fealty.

The mounted warrior, garbed in chainmail, sat firmly on a saddle with stirrups, from where he could control his horse and wield lance, axe or sword. So long as the knights fought a fixed enemy, they were invincible, but against a mobile enemy who struck from afar with arrows or who could outmanoeuvre them or avoid them, they were almost helpless. Thus the European powers dependent on knights (unlike the organised Byzantine Empire of the east) were incapable of stopping the depredations of Muslim pirates or the highly mobile armies of the Magyars (like the Huns, a nomadic people from the east) who, for almost a century (862–954), raided Western Europe at will. The kings of Europe relied on fortifications until in 955 at Augsburg and the Lech River, Otto I ('the Great') cornered the Magyar army, forcing them to fight his kind of battle – hand-to-hand at close quarters – and destroyed them. As a consequence of this victory, in 962 the Pope anointed Otto emperor of a new Holy Roman Empire.

Even more dangerous than Muslim pirates and the Magyars were the Vikings. Their combination of a low-draught, ocean-going ship which could navigate any river, beach on any shore, be portaged and launched easily bow or stern first, carried the Vikings everywhere in Europe. The fierce crews, bred and trained in the warlike environment of Scandinavia, were unstoppable. They had already occupied the major river routes through Russia – the name 'Russia' derives from the Rus, the original invaders from Scandinavia – and they travelled all the way down the rivers to the Black Sea and to Constantinople where they formed an elite imperial guard, the Varangians. Their berserker onslaughts, so successful against the military forces of their age, were precisely the sort of attack the Roman legions had been formed to withstand.

Through the ninth and tenth centuries, the Vikings raided the western coasts of Europe, entered the Mediterranean, raided as far east as Italy and penetrated inland to Paris. They established kingdoms in Ireland and France and, in 1066 under the leadership of William the Conqueror of Normandy, they invaded England, defeated the Anglo-Saxon king at the battle of Hastings and founded a new kingdom. Normans also established kingdoms in Italy and Sicily. Gradually, however, the attacking, pagan Vikings evolved into local Christian defenders.

At the end of the eleventh century with much of Scandinavia converted to Christianity and the church in moral ascendancy, Pope Urban II called upon Christian realms to unite for a crusade to free Jerusalem and the Holy Lands and, in the process, to rescue the Christian kingdom of the east, Byzantium.

The wars of the Crusades (1096–1291), begun with the occupation of the Holy Land in the First Crusade, matched the heavily armed and armoured cavalry of Europe against the light cavalry of the Islamic world (centred in Egypt). If the eastern cavalry stood and fought, the European cavalry from its first devastating charge to its prowess in the melee had an overwhelming advantage but, as Muslim leaders learned European tactics, they altered their own and tried to avoid the first charge and take advantage of their manoeuvrable light cavalry to strike from a distance. In turn, the Crusaders changed from a military culture in which only the knight mattered to a more balanced force of cavalry and infantry. Still, their leaders continued to suffer from their cultural emphasis on the knight and the conviction that one good charge would win the battle.

> No animal is more noble than the horse, since it is by horses that princes, magnates and knights are separated from lesser people, and because a lord cannot fittingly be seen among private citizens except through the mediation of a horse.[2]

On the whole, the Crusades did considerable damage to Christendom. During the Fourth Crusade (1198–1204) the Franks attacked and conquered the Byzantine Empire in Greece. When they were finally driven out, the Byzantine Empire was no longer able to defend itself against the Muslim powers and, in 1453, Constantinople itself fell to the Ottoman Turks. The Turks occupied and ruled Greece for almost four centuries after that.

Another effect of the Crusades in the West was the recognition of the centrality and influence of the church. The church offered purpose and direction: to recover lands from Islam (Spain); to advance Christianity into eastern Europe (Poland, Prussia, Russia); and to give legitimacy to kings and kingdoms. By 1200 the Holy Roman Empire, founded in the tenth century, encompassed most of central Europe and northern Italy.

The Hundred Years' War (1337–1457) between France and England, and the many dynastic wars and the wars between contending and independent Italian cities, transformed warfare – and also civilisation – at the beginning of the Renaissance (1400–1550).

In the battle of Agincourt (25 October 1415) Henry V and a mixed force of 5,000–6,000 English longbow men and 1,000 knights defeated a superior French force (approximately 25,000 foot and horse). Henry was intercepted by a French army as he was marching to Calais and forced to fight. Henry ordered his archers to fire and, in response, the French launched an attack. The English bowmen broke up the mounted attack, but the French infantry reached the English lines, fought hand-to-hand in an intense melee and finally withdrew with heavy losses. Henry, uncertain whether he would be attacked again, ordered all the prisoners killed. The French withdrew.

The importance of this battle is not reflected in the total number of troops involved – Alexander the Great had more men in his own army at the battle of Gaugamela.[3] Agincourt stands out as an amazing victory of firepower (the longbow) over a superior force of knights, but it was far from decisive and Henry's son, Henry VI, continued fighting in France to establish his claim to the French crown. His war culminated with the siege of Orleans, the last holdout of the French loyalists. Both sides used cannon in this siege and, after a year, the French were worn down and on the verge of capitulation, when a simple 18-year-old girl, Joan of Arc, armed with the belief that she had been chosen by God to save France, inspired the French heir to the throne and his army to fight on. First, in 1429, she oversaw the provisioning of the starving garrison of Orleans and then she participated in the series of assaults which lifted the siege. Her presence alone, as the instrument of heaven, gave Charles legitimacy and divine sanction as the new king of France. In 1452, two decades after her death, the French finally drove the last English from France.

As weapons evolved and tactics changed, thoughtful men – who had read classical authors and recognised the potency of Caesar's army – sought advice in one particular ancient author, Vegetius. Vegetius wrote in the late fourth century or the early fifth century AD. His work, *de re militari* (or *epitome rei militaris*) looked back to the classical Roman legion with the purpose of informing his audience of the deficiencies of the army of his own time and what should be done about it. Vegetius was an important author in the Middle Ages (earliest manuscript tenth or eleventh century) and Renaissance; Richard the Lionhearted (r. 1189–99) had a copy[4] and Vegetius was still considered important as late as 1770 when an Austrian field marshal claimed that 'Vegetius had been inspired by God'.[5]

They realised that no contemporary army approached the efficiency and capabilities of the Roman army – its ability to move long distances, to transport supplies, to engineer pathways through forest, mountain, and swamp, to bridge rivers, to maintain a road system and to deliver an army fed and rested to a battlefield far distant from Rome – but, equally so, leaders wanted to achieve these qualities and they believed a study of classical authors could help. Into the fifteenth century a Roman legionary army could have met any army on the field of battle, held its own and, with competent leadership, prevailed. Not until the time of Napoleon did armies match the Roman armies in size, in discipline and in logistics. Nonetheless, the development of gunpowder weapons in the fifteenth century introduced a new epoch in warfare.

The Chinese invented gunpowder sometime in the ninth century (or earlier). The first evidence for the use of gunpowder in projectile weapons comes from a sculpture of the twelfth century; the first actual gun unearthed by archaeologists dates to the thirteenth century.[6] The formula for gunpowder had been brought to Europe in the first half of the thirteenth century by visitors returning from the Mongol court; one of the visitors, a Franciscan friend of Roger Bacon (1214–94), gave him the formula and Bacon introduced it to a wider European audience.[7]

The year 1326 is the earliest record of the use of firearms in Europe (though they must have been invented and developed earlier) – two

Florentine magistrates were charged with the task of obtaining firearms to defend Florence. The development of firearms coincided with the increasing importance of infantry. By the end of the fourteenth century cannon had been used to breach a besieged city's walls.[8]

Between the 1320s, when the first 'cannon' is described, and the later 1400s – that is, during the Hundred Years War (1337–1453) – the wrought iron, stone throwing 'bombard' became the premiere weapon of siege warfare, knocking breaches in the walls of the English forts in France and the Byzantine Constantinople, which fell to the Turks in 1453. Cannon put every wall at risk, but they were, and remained, too heavy and too cumbersome to be used effectively on the battlefield, until improved gunpowder made possible individual guns – first the arquebus and then the musket – fired from a Y-support implanted in the ground. The penetrating power of the musket's projectile rendered armour obsolete.

By the 1490s the French had developed a new cannon, a bronze-cast tube, no more than eight feet long, which fired an iron cannon ball[9] and was light enough to be transported with an army. In 1494 the king of France, Charles VIII, using a siege train of 40 guns, conquered Italy from Florence to Naples in one campaign. He was driven out before the end of the century by an alliance of Spain, Venice and the Holy Roman Empire but, nonetheless, his campaign proved that cannon could knock down traditional fortifications and his success ushered in the 'age of artillery'. (To suggest how innovative cannon were, many towns up to this time had sheltered safely behind walls built by the Romans – although repaired and renewed since.) The French cannon became the main artillery piece of armies for the next four centuries.

The last decade of the fifteenth century saw the beginning of a shift in world power. In 1492 the Spanish drove out the last Muslims and Columbus discovered America. The Portuguese began the European domination of India and the Spanish, under the leadership of Cortes and Pizarro, defeated the best organised Indian nations of the New World and established Spanish empires.

In the face of the new threat from artillery, European cities undertook an intense effort to create new fortifications, or to modify old fortifications. The necessity for new fortifications opened a new field of military architecture and engineering which attracted such diverse talents as Leonardo da Vinci (1451–1519) and Michelangelo. The engineers first tried an immediate solution; to bolster the walls with earthworks, which cannon balls would penetrate and not destroy, but they soon turned to a better solution: the bastion – a stone- and earth-filled barrier with sloping walls and sharp angles, deep enough both to diminish the impact of cannon balls and also to furnish a platform on which the besieged could mount their own cannon.

The engineers first made defence equal to the offence and then superior to it, but the resources they required to build the bastions could come only from an organised state, that is, usually, a king who, at the same time, could assure his dominance within his realm by thwarting towns from building their own bastions. One historian observes, 'The modern frontiers of Europe are, indeed, largely the outcome of fortress building . . .'[10]

By the beginning of the sixteenth century commanders had already organised their armies into units of different arms. In addition to the cavalry, still the prestigious arm, they added units of archers (the longbow, if English), crossbowmen and pike men. The Swiss redeveloped the pike phalanx which could withstand a cavalry charge – if the phalanx held fast – and served as mercenary units throughout Europe for centuries (and still guard the Pope). Commanders were beginning to replace their crossbow men with individual gunners. The transition was easy in concept – a small, light cannon barrel was placed on a crossbow frame – and initially the unit of gunners was employed like a unit of crossbow men.

In the battle of Ravenna (1512) – part of the attempt of the French to control northern Italy – the two sides exchanged artillery fire for the first time in history . . . for about two hours. In the battle of Marignano (1515) – in a campaign by Francis I of France – Swiss pike men charged the French battery of 72 guns and drove the gunners off, but were then themselves repulsed. They continued to skirmish through the night and in the morning the Swiss again charged the battery. The Swiss suffered horrific casualties as the French held their own until French allies – the Venetians – arrived, and the allies could force the Swiss from the field. These two battles proved the effectiveness of cannon on the battlefield for once and all. The effectiveness of hand-gunners was established at the battle of Bicocca in 1522, when a force of 3,000 Swiss infantry were annihilated in an attack on a fortified position guarded by hand-gunners.

Military leaders had to acknowledge now that gunpowder had revolutionised tactics on the battlefield, that an assault on a fortified position guarded by individual gunners would devastate the attacking force, that, therefore, they had to rethink their very concept of war and what they knew about fighting a battle and, finally and sadly (for them), that they had to accept the truth of one knight's lament, 'What is the use, any more, of the skill-at-arms of the knights [...] when such weapons may be used in war?'[11]

By the end of the sixteenth century the armoured knight was gone, replaced by light cavalry and infantry (gunners and pike men combined). Throughout Europe, while cavalry still carried prestige and was still an integral part of an army, the main and indispensable arm was the infantry and, to the commanders and theorists, the premiere infantry in all of history were the legions of Julius Caesar.

When the Dutch Protestants rebelled from the Catholic Spanish in 1566, they relied on their fortification to wear down and wear out the Spanish. The Spanish could not sustain the financial strain nor the strain put on their troops in the sieges – a lot of digging followed by an extremely dangerous assault. By 1590 the Dutch, under their commander Count Maurice of Nassau, were able to assume the offensive against the Spanish and compel them to agree to a truce in 1608. Maurice had developed a drill manual based on Vegetius.[12] He reorganised his army along 'Roman' lines, dividing it into 550-man battalions (like cohorts), the battalions into companies and the companies into platoons. His commanding general thereby could issue orders which would travel down to the lowliest private who could thus carry out his orders more quickly.

Maurice also had his army build an entrenched camp every night. He commissioned the gun-works to make lighter, more mobile cannon and he reorganised and increased the number of musketeers. His musketeers were trained to perform automatically the 42 steps of reloading and he instituted a formation five-deep, so that the front rank could fire on command, about face, and retreat through the formation, reloading as they went. Each subsequent front line would fire and retreat, so that his formation could maintain a continuous fire on the enemy. He also trained his pike men so that in the face of a cavalry charge, they could open their ranks and admit the retreating musketeers. He founded the first military academy in Europe. His example affected every army in Europe. His cousin John, inspired by the ancient author, Aelian, further developed the manual of arms and the two created uniforms for their special units, because the Romans had had uniforms.[13]

By the mid-sixteenth century (and until the French Revolution) Europe was riven by the rivalries of royal dynasties, the most powerful of which was the Hapsburg dynasty. The Holy Roman Empire existed in name only. Poland was the largest kingdom in Europe, the Ottoman Empire reached almost to Vienna and leaders studied and mastered the tactics of land warfare.

In naval warfare, however, strategic concepts had hardly changed since the anonymous author, known as the 'Old Oligarch', wrote his essay on the subject in the 420s BC. In the Mediterranean Sea in the sixteenth century, fleets of Ottoman and Christian galleys fought much as galleys had always fought, manoeuvring to ram or, now, to bring a bow-placed cannon to bear. Archers on board the Ottoman vessels gave them a formidable advantage until the battle of Lepanto (1571) when the Christian fleet used firearms to repel boarders and inflict casualties of 50 per cent on the Ottomans.

Ocean-going vessels were more able to take advantage of cannon to develop new battle tactics. The Europeans with fighting ships under sail and troops with firearms established themselves on the coasts of all the rest of the world, and from the coasts conquered or dominated the hinterland. The European fleets had no rivals outside the Mediterranean except other European fleets, but the disputes on land were carried over to the oceans.

The most famous confrontation between European sea forces was the attempt of Spain to conquer England when, in 1588, the Spanish Armada suffered a catastrophic defeat. For the better part of the seventeenth century Europeans fought each other for pieces of the new (to them) world.

The first great tactical innovator of the new army was Gustavus Adolphus, king of Sweden (r. 1611–32). The king's heroes were Maurice of Nassau, Xenophon (the hero of the *Anabasis*) and Hugo Grotius. (Napoleon said that Gustavus Adolphus was 'animated by the principles of Alexander, Hannibal and Caesar'.[14]) He recognised the new efficiency of the musket – the primitive matchlock had been replaced with the more reliable flint striker, the pike man had been replaced by the soldier wielding a bayoneted musket and mercenaries were being replaced with local recruits (as advised by Machiavelli in his treatise on war in 1521 – in it he had recommended the conscription, training and organisation of local troops as though they were Roman, basing his theories on the work of Vegetius).[15] These changes, he believed, necessitated the reorganisation of the army and the introduction of new tactics.

Gustavus Adolphus recognised that a king had to develop a new relationship with his national army. He had to lead by example and he had to see to their wellbeing, not just to boost their morale, but to ensure that they were fit to fight. He broke with past conventions and did what the necessities of the new weapons required. Gustavus Adolphus lightened his artillery and reduced his baggage train so that his army could move faster. His tactics in battle were simple: to punish and confuse the enemy with his artillery and then to launch his cavalry through the smoke screen of powder, disrupt the enemy formations and scatter them, at which point he would order his infantry to advance.

The Swedish king entered Europe to defend Sweden by waging an aggressive war outside its borders (the Thirty Years War). In the conflicting alliances and double-dealing, he brought his principal Catholic enemy to battle at Breitenfeld in 1631. The two armies confronted each other and fired their cannon, but Gustavus Adolphus had many more pieces and by their fire caused the premature charge of the enemy cavalry and advance of the enemy left. Gustavus Adolphus' allies were broken, but the king launched an attack on the enemies' unprotected flank and routed the enemy army. The Battle of Breitenfeld has been called the 'first modern battle' because it was won by manoeuvre and firepower.[16]

In the spring, Gustavus Adolphus advanced on the Rhine with the intention of uniting the Protestant lands of Germany against the Catholic lands across the Rhine and the Danube. In 1632, after a summer of manoeuvres, the enemy divided their troops in winter quarters, but Gustavus Adolphus advanced on the main force at Lützen and prepared to force a battle. The two armies approached each other in heavy mist and Gustavus Adolphus used the cover of the mist to attack and rout the enemy left flank. In the mist, however, he fell in with a party of the enemy, who killed him. His men, infuriated by the news of his death, advanced and in brutal fighting broke the enemy's formations. With the death of Gustavus Adolphus the Thirty Years War degenerated into a purposeless slaughter of the people of central Europe until its end in 1648.

By the end of the 1600s, infantry on the battlefield consisted almost entirely of musket-bearing soldiers who fired their muskets, affixed bayonets and then fought as pike men. Along with the universal adoption of the musket came also the drill. Soldiers were trained in the manual of arms to load their muskets, raise them to their shoulders, level them as ordered and fire volleys on command. Every action was broken into its constituent parts and practised until it was automatic. The desired effect of the drill was to protect the ranks against themselves through premature discharge and to steady them on a battlefield so that they could load in the face of hostile fire.

Units of infantry were enlisted, uniformed, trained and disciplined (often through flogging) until they could act without thinking. Their officers, drawn from the gentry, likewise had to undergo training and, consequently, the first military academies were founded in this century with a curriculum heavily based upon the classics and, in particular, on the Roman concepts of training and practice. Artillery officers and engineers also studied mathematics. Battles in Europe were fought between similar armies using similar tactics: field artillery firing into the opposing ranks; infantry facing infantry and enduring volley upon volley of musket fire; and cavalry waiting for an opportunity to charge into a disorganised enemy.

Between the end of the Thirty Years War in 1648 and the accession of Frederick the Great in 1740, Prussia formed into a state, became a rival to France (which under Louis XIV threatened to dominate the whole of Western Europe and the New World) and was a force among the states of Poland, Russia and Austria. Its power was based on an army conscripted from the free men of Prussia and officered by nobles required to pass through military schools. Frederick, upon his accession, had at his disposal an army of about 80,000 men. He used this army to interfere in the succession to the throne of Austria and thereby acquire the territory of Silesia. In a series of battles, with mixed victories and defeats, he forced the European powers to recognise his claims in the peace of 1748.

Over the course of time Frederick developed a simple tactical scheme based on the mobility of his army. In a time of slow-moving armies, Frederick was able to attack his enemies before they were prepared or, if they occupied the battlefield, to manoeuvre against their flank and roll the enemy army up through a combination of shock and fire. His army, he claimed, could fire at a rate three times that of his enemy and his artillery was equally quick to come into action. On the other hand, his impetuosity often brought him into situations he could not control and, eventually, he was forced to accept that battles and wars did not bring the security he expected. Nonetheless, he lived in a time when kings were expected to fight battles and he continued his aggressive policy until he forced a hostile alliance of France, Austria, Sweden, Saxony and Russia. During the Seven Years War (1756–63) Frederick won and lost battles, saw Berlin occupied and freed again and finally guided his kingdom, united and strong, through to the end of the war.

Frederick introduced the oblique attack, rapid movement, horse artillery and effective mass musketry. Nonetheless, he did not hold any considerable edge over his enemies' armies and his battles were slaughter grounds where disciplined ranks suffered cannon fire and discharged volleys of musket balls into each other. Frederick said, 'If my soldiers began to think, not one would remain in the ranks'.[17] Despite his tactical abilities and the innovations that preceded him, his wars and the wars before Napoleon tended to be those with indecisive battles, many sieges and multiple skirmishes across the belligerent nations.[18] On the other hand, European armies, trained in this discipline, found themselves superior to the other armies of the world and were able to push the Ottoman Empire back.

The American Revolution, followed by the French Revolution, created a citizen army which, in the American Revolution, became a national symbol. George Washington recognised that as long as he could maintain his citizen army, he was maintaining a nation. The British commanders, although competent enough to defeat the Americans in the field, were never able to put together a comprehensive strategy to win the war. They struggled to find a way to fight the American militia, which used their rifles to strike at the British from a distant cover – British officers were so outraged by this style of warfare that one said, 'A rifleman is not entitled to any quarter'.[19] In the end the American citizen army prevailed.

In France the revolution, by curtailing the power of the aristocracy, led first to the rise of Napoleon Bonaparte,[20] second to the creation of the national army by conscription – for the first time in over 1,000 years armies were larger than Roman armies – and third, to an officer corps open to all talents – some of the best French marshals began their careers in the ranks. Junior officers, through a combination of the experience of a long war and a wide-open selection process, became the best officer corps in Europe.

The citizen army required its commanders to adapt. The recruits were unable to master the extensive and intricate manoeuvres of the heavily trained and disciplined troops of the monarchy, neither to charge the enemy in line nor to stand and receive fire while they loaded, aimed and fired back, so the commanders developed new tactics which took advantage of the high morale of the citizen-soldiers while not requiring as much training. The commanders deployed skirmishers to engage the enemy with fire while their artillery opened lanes in the enemy lines and then, at the first sign of weakness, they ordered the main body of French infantry to charge the enemy in columns. Casualties were high but the mass of men overwhelmed the enemy. The attack in columns could not succeed, however, without the effective deployment of artillery.

Napoleon was a student of war. He had trained in the artillery, had continued to study artillery practice and he had commanded artillery in battles and sieges. Before a campaign he would have the national library send him every book it had on the region. He would pore over the maps and imagine marching an army from one site to another, and he would estimate how long it would take. Moreover his army, unlike other European armies with long supply trains, would set out with three days' rations. He expected his men to live off the land and, as a consequence, he was able to move more quickly than his enemies.

During the course of his first campaigns in Italy he developed a technique which he used over and over again: he would force his army into the middle of the enemy armies or between divisions of the same army and then from a central position strike out at one flank or the other, keeping the enemy off balance. Eventually his enemies learned by fighting him and by studying his campaigns to develop similar armies and similar tactics; as often happens in a prolonged war, they became his equal.

In the meantime, however, Napoleon defeated all his enemies, one after another. He was the first to be able to achieve decisive victory in a battle fought with firearms. His national army vastly outnumbered the forces of the enemy monarchies; in battle it overwhelmed and scattered its enemy and, in western Europe, could pursue them until they ran out of space and time to regroup. In Russia, however, in 1812, Napoleon fought an enemy which had room to flee and regroup and flee and regroup again; Russian tenacity and the brutal Russian winter caused Napoleon's first – and catastrophic – defeat.

Before the defeat in Russia, however, Britain had used its fleet to protect the British Isles, to attack the French where it could and to give support to its allies. With control of the seas, the British were able to support a campaign on the periphery of the French Empire in Portugal and Spain (the Peninsular Campaign) under the command of Wellington. Wellington defeated the French and, after the disastrous campaign in Russia, pressed north, while the reconstituted Prussian army and the Russian army pressed west. At last, cornered in France, Napoleon accepted the inevitable and offered to abdicate.

Napoleon was exiled to the island of Elba, but he returned to France (the campaign of the Hundred Days). He won several victories and was within a couple of hours of catching the Duke of Wellington and perhaps defeating him, but was stopped by a thunderstorm. Nonetheless, he was determined to fight Wellington before the Prussians could join him; he pressed on after him and brought him to battle at Waterloo on 18 June 1815.

The battlefield was a plain between two ridges (occupied by the opposing armies) and bisected by a road parallel to the ridges. Wellington strengthened his army to the west because he expected the Prussians to come from the east. He stationed advanced forces in the plain to disrupt the anticipated French attacks on his position. Napoleon delayed his attack until the early afternoon to give the ground a chance to dry out enough to support his artillery and cavalry. He believed the Prussian army was too far away and too slow to reach the battlefield that day.

Napoleon's plan was simple, if not clear to his subordinates. He launched an attack on the advanced forces of the British to his left (Wellington's right) to divert troops from Wellington's centre upon which Napoleon intended to launch his main attack. This attack failed to achieve its objective and his artillery was ineffective.

Napoleon's main attack, despite significant losses from artillery fire, crested the ridge and for one critical moment appeared to have won the battle. However, Napoleon had not advanced his cavalry and he could not exploit the success before British cavalry and infantry counterattacked, broke up the French attack and drove them back. Napoleon then had to decide whether to retreat or to try once more to break the British before the Prussians arrived. He ordered another attack. In this attack his cavalry advanced without artillery or infantry support and under heavy British artillery fire; the French charged the British lines, which formed in squares, eight times but failed to break them, although the attack forced Wellington to commit all his reserves and all his cavalry.

It was now late afternoon and the first Prussian division had launched its attack on Napoleon's right flank so that he was forced to detach troops to stop the Prussians but, nonetheless, the 'Old Guard' under Marshall Ney launched yet another attack on the British centre and this time was on the verge of a breakthrough, but Napoleon did not support him in time, one last attempt failed and the French began to retreat as the Prussian army entered the battle. Wellington then ordered his army to advance with bayonets and routed the French army. In truth, the battle of Waterloo was won by British courage, Wellington's leadership and the Prussians' determination to reach the battlefield, while Napoleon lost control of the elements of his army, which attacked piecemeal or did not get into the battle at all. Napoleon died in exile.

In the aftermath of such a long and ruinous war, European leaders met in Vienna – at the Congress of Vienna – to settle the issues raised by the war: they reorganised the Holy Roman Empire into a Confederation of German States; they gave the Rhineland to Prussia; they divided Poland; and they granted independence to the Low Countries. The Congress of Vienna established borders and a general peace which, by and large, lasted for a century from 1815 to 1914, although the balance of power shifted as Prussia united Germany and defeated France in the Franco-Prussian War (1870–1).

Another result of the war was a renewed study of strategy, tactics and theory. Carl von Clausewitz studied Napoleon and the French national army and developed a theory of war: the age of total war, nation against nation, had arrived and, therefore, leaders must now consider war as part of political action. His ideas were absorbed by the German general staff and leaders who used them to achieve national unity and defeat France in 1871; other European political leaders and generals accepted Clausewitz's ideas not by deliberate study, but in a slow process as his theories evolved into a world view. They were slower to recognise how the battlefield had been changed by improved artillery and accurate and swift rifle fire.

In the major wars of the nineteenth century antiquity left its legacy in covert ways – the leaders all studied Caesar, for instance – but in the war of Greek Independence antiquity had a direct effect. Educated Europeans had a particular connection with Greece – 'We are all Greeks', Shelley said – albeit the Greece of Pericles, Plato, Aristotle and Homer.[21] Few educated Europeans had actual experience with Greeks, and the many who went to fight for Greek independence had their illusions shattered. Nonetheless, in the end, those feelings of cultural heritage freed Greece.

For a minor conflict there were some notable innovations. On 20 April 1827 in the Gulf of Volo, for the first time a steam-powered iron-hulled warship, the *Karteria*, puffed into the port, attacked eight Turkish ships, captured five, burned two and destroyed the eighth with gunfire; and for the last time two fleets 'under sail' (one was anchored) fought a battle in the bay of Navarino on 20 October 1827, establishing Greek independence.[22]

Once again military technology was racing ahead of generals' understanding. By the end of the American Civil War the lessons were there for anyone who wished to see. The United States had, first, an enormous material and economic advantage over the Confederacy. Second, it had a system of rapid transportation – the railroad (which the Germans studied and used to advantage in the Franco-Prussian War), and third, it had an advantage in numbers of soldiers. Nonetheless, given the nature of the new rifles, the casualties were high. (More Americans were killed in the Civil War than in any other war Americans have fought, and more Americans were killed in one day at Antietam than in any other battle.) Cavalry proved impotent against steady infantry and developed into a mobile force which would ride to the scene of action and then dismount to fight. Artillery, when well used, was decisive. Casualties in the assault were so high that generals accepted that they could take a defended position only when they outnumbered the defensive force at the point of attack by four to one. The United States initiated conscription, mass production of uniforms and weapons and a logistical system. It encouraged military invention and innovation and built the first all-iron warship.

This ship, the *Monitor*, met the iron-clad *Merrimac* in the first battle between iron-clad, steam-powered warships. Herman Melville wrote a poem about it.[23]

> The ringing of those plates on plates
> Still ringeth round the world;
> War yet shall be, but warriors
> Are now but operatives.

The Union strategy of dividing and reducing the South was temporarily thwarted by the brilliant leadership of Robert E. Lee and the élan of southern troops, but steady leadership and the relentless pursuit of its strategy gradually constrained the South and compelled Robert E. Lee to gamble that an invasion of the North might tip the scales. In the summer of 1863 he invaded Pennsylvania and encountered the Union army at Gettysburg. Neither side had expected to fight a battle there and both sides rushed to seize critical terrain.

Time and again individual Union commanders identified, seized and held what proved to be the key points of the battlefield. Wisconsin troops on Culps' Hill beat off a Confederate attack which would have turned the whole Union army. Maine troops, defending Little Round Top, beat off several attacks, but they ran out of ammunition and they could hear the Confederates massing for another attack; their commander told them to fix bayonets and led them down the hill in a charge that broke up the rebel forces and saved this absolutely critical position.

When Robert E. Lee tried one last assault – Pickett's charge – on the Union position across an open field, Pickett's command was destroyed by Union artillery. In the ensuing campaign the Union army, under the command of the newly appointed Ulysses S. Grant, clung to the army of Robert E. Lee while another Union army under Tecumseh Sherman defeated the Confederate forces in the west and then marched through the South in a demonstration of the helplessness of the Confederacy. Robert E. Lee was finally caught between these two armies and he surrendered at the Appomattox Court House in 1865.

The American Civil War was a devastating demonstration of the new power of cannon and rifles, but European staff officers believed that it had little to teach them and later even discounted the effect that the machine gun would have on battle. (Hiram Maxim's 1884 machine gun could fire 600 bullets a minute.) The generals and political leaders, totally unprepared for the effects of these weapons, stumbled blindly into World War I although, it must be said, ordinary citizens, who were as ignorant as their leaders, were eager for war and ready to serve in their countries' armed forces. The German author, Ernst Jünger, described himself as being 'enraptured by war'.[24] In England, fuelled by heroic tales of creating and holding empires, most notably by Rudyard Kipling, many young men agreed with Rupert Brooke,

> Now God be thanked Who has matched us with His hour,
> And caught our youth, and wakened us from sleeping.[25]

Opinions changed with experience, of course. A war initially of movement soon devolved in the West into trench warfare. Hundreds of thousands of young men on both sides rose from the trenches and advanced into a hail of small arms, machine gun and artillery fire. Thousands died as the generals sought a decisive battle through larger assaults, more artillery, mining, poison gas and, finally, tanks. (The battle of Verdun in 1916 had 1 million casualties, the battle of the Somme in 1916, 1 million casualties and the third battle of Ypres in 1917, 500,000 casualties.)

The Germans, constrained by a two-front war, held their own in the West while in the East they conducted a war of movement, knocked Russia out of the war – and into revolution – and then transferred their troops west and their method of attack, a swift and precise artillery barrage to isolate the battlefield followed by an assault of specially trained troops. The effect on the allies was devastating, but the assault could not be sustained in the face of growing American reinforcements. New Allied attacks pushed the Germans out into open country and kept forcing them to retreat until they realised that they could not win the war and they accepted an armistice and the subsequent peace. The mediocre leaders who had led their nations into war proved no better in arranging the peace. They recognised no fault in themselves, put all the blame on Germany and sowed the seeds of World War II in the Treaty of Versailles

The losses of World War I were so horrific that the French and British recoiled from any prospect of another war like it. The poet Wilfred Owen, killed in the war, left a line that summed up general feelings: 'The old lie: *Dulce et decorum est/Pro patria mori*'. ('It is sweet to die for one's country'.)[26] Nations outlawed the use of poison gas – and, by and large, up to the present time, have adhered to their agreement – but a new weapon, the aeroplane, once again revolutionised war.

An aeroplane could fly over the English Channel, bomb British cities and, although the capacity of air power to bomb precisely and to win wars by itself was exaggerated, its ability to deliver destruction and terror was not. In addition, the Germans linked fighter-bombers with armoured divisions to operate as independent units spearheading assaults, which they called *blitzkrieg*. While the concept of *blitzkrieg* was at least as old as Alexander the Great – break through at a weak spot, disrupt the enemy army, send part of it in flight and then spread confusion and panic in the rear – now, with radio communications and the speed of motorised vehicles, the Germans were able to advance far enough and quickly enough to cut off whole armies.

While the British and French had learned to abhor the uniform and military service, the Germans embraced it. Hitler could say at the beginning of the invasion of Poland in 1939, 'I have once more put on the coat that was most sacred and dear to me'.[27] In 1940 the German *blitzkrieg* shattered the French defensive line and defeated the French in a single summer, but the Germans failed to knock England out of the war with their air force and began planning for an invasion – Operation Sea Lion. The Germans studied previous successful invaders: Julius Caesar, the emperor Claudius and William the Conqueror.[28] (The allies also studied the same campaigns to prepare for their invasion of the continent.) When Hitler lost the Battle of Britain he decided to invade Russia. After an initial spectacular advance, the Germans were stopped by the winter and then bogged down by the vast spaces and the dogged resistance of the Russians.

In Asia, the Japanese acted on their belief that their expansion into the Orient was unfairly circumscribed by the United States' refusal to allow them access to the sources of petroleum their armed forces needed and, on 7 December 1941, the Japanese launched a surprise attack on Pearl Harbour. The Japanese attack missed the aircraft carriers which had put to sea and, of course, it could not strike at American production.

The war in the Pacific was defined by the new necessities of naval warfare, transformed by the aeroplane from the duel of battleships to the duel of aircraft launched from aircraft carriers. Battles were fought beyond gun range and without ship sighting ship. At the battle of Midway, American aircraft sank four Japanese aircraft carriers and turned the tide of the war; the American fleet advanced against isolated Japanese outposts which, while defended to the last man, nonetheless had no chance against the locally overwhelming force. Still, despite new technology and changing tactics, the war was a series of battles which brought the allied forces ever closer to the homelands of Germany, Italy and Japan. Italy was knocked out of the war first and then, with allied forces converging inside Germany itself and the suicide of Adolf Hitler, Germany surrendered.

Faced with the estimated casualties of an invasion of Japan, the President of the United States, Harry S. Truman, authorised the use of two atomic bombs against the Japanese. At the time the decision seemed to be tactical and not moral. Ever since, the full horror of nuclear fallout and death by radiation has kept the weapon from being used again. The bombings of Hiroshima and Nagasaki, however, accomplished their purpose – the Japanese capitulated.

World War II was a total war using all the resources of the belligerent nations brought against soldier and civilian alike. A British air force directive of 14 February 1942 stated that air operations should 'be focused on the morale of the enemy civilian population . . .'[29]

The end of World War II did not bring peace. The Soviet Union occupied Eastern Europe and the United States and western European nations formed a military alliance whose unstated enemy was the Soviet Union. The Cold War lasted from the end of World War II to the fall of the Soviet Union in 1990. Added to the prospect that any war between the major powers would result in total war was the new prospect that war would include an exchange of nuclear weapons. The United States and the Soviet Union worked out a *modus vivendi* of mutual assured destruction if they employed nuclear weapons against each other. Consequently, for 45 years they supported surrogates in the Cold War – the Korean War, the Vietnam War and the Soviet Afghan War were confined to one territory with limited objectives, thus allowing Soviets and Americans to avoid direct confrontation.

In the twenty-first century the United States has developed true precision bombing and, since Vietnam, has had an all-volunteer armed force. Most European countries have also shifted to a professional army. The weapons of modern war have changed, but the organisation of the military services and war itself would be readily recognisable to Greeks and Romans. The basic questions faced by each society – Who should command and who should serve? What is the place of the military in society? What justifies war? Who decides to go to war? – have not changed. Nor have the basic principles of war changed.

The unit with which the author served in Vietnam has also served in Afghanistan – the First of the Twenty-Seventh Infantry (Wolfhounds). On its flag appears the Latin motto, *Nec Aspera Terrent*, which soldiers translate as 'No Fear On Earth'.

CHAPTER IV

THE STUDY OF WAR

'Syria Accused of Crimes Against Humanity by UN Panel'.
London – A United Nations panel concluded Thursday that 'gross human rights violations' had been ordered by the Syrian authorities as a matter of state policy, amounting to crimes against humanity.

New York Times, Friday 24 February 2012

The United Nations panel that concluded that Syria had violated international law based its judgement on the results of debates about war and justice initiated more than 2,500 years ago by Greek and Roman thinkers.

The world's first historian, the Greek Herodotus, wrote, 'No one is stupid enough to prefer war to peace; in peace sons bury their fathers and in war fathers bury their sons. However, I suppose some god must have wanted this to happen'.[1]

Greeks believed that war was the normal condition of human existence. Plato's Cretan speaker in the *Laws* says,

> It seems to me that [the lawgiver] had contempt for the mass of people who did not understand that every city is at war continually against every other city [...] and for that reason must incorporate the discipline and organisation for war into their everyday life. Peace is just a word, since all nations are by nature constantly at war – although a kind of undeclared war – with all other nations [...] and the lawgiver

arranged the laws to guard [the State], for nothing else matters at all, neither possessions or private lives, without the mastery of war, because the victors possess all of the good things of the defeated.[2]

The Cretan continues that, just as every city is constantly at war with every other city, so, too, is every village at war with every other village, and every house, and even every man within himself to gain control of himself![3] Plato, in response, as the 'Athenian stranger', proposes that, just as the best condition for a single man is that his better nature rule and that he be in harmony with himself, so, too, should each household, village and city be in harmony with itself and, furthermore, he proposed that the very best condition would be that all cities were at peace with all other cities.

Mankind, however, has not always lived in a world at war. The earliest philosophers, persuaded by Hesiod's *Works and Days*,[4] believed that mankind first lived in a simple primeval society, superior to our own, a golden age when golden men lived without growing old or knowing misery and they died as though they were falling asleep. They were succeeded by the inferior silver men and they by the bronze men who loved war and fought each other until they all perished. The bronze men were succeeded by the heroes who, despite their love of battle, were honoured by Zeus and sent upon their deaths to the Isles of the Blest.

Finally, Zeus made the present generation, the men of iron who 'never stop from weariness and pain during the day and at night they die'.[5] In his age, the modern age, Hesiod writes, strife and competition (Eris) are constant, although one type of strife is good and leads men to work harder for themselves and thus to prosper, while the other type is bad and causes war.[6] They – we! – are a violent race among whom all that matters is force.

The Stoics accepted Hesiod's view of human nature, and in their doctrine they identify strife, or rivalry, as the reason that justice must be put first in a community, to balance (or harmonise) human nature:[7]

Everything was created for the use of men; men, however, were created for the sake of other men, that they themselves could make provision for each other; in nature we follow a leader, who forces us to put communal things in the middle, to exchange duties, and to give and receive; then civilisation tamed mankind through his own intelligence and the arts [...] but all depended first upon justice [...] [because] [...] justice is the first principle, to ensure that no one suffers an injury, unless he has injured another. The second principle is that the common things are used for the community, while private things belong to private individuals. Individuals do not own property in nature – property is considered 'owned' either by long-standing occupation, that is, that someone in the past occupied vacant land or had conquered land in some war, or, second, by legal means.[8]

Cicero's contemporary, Lucretius, presents the Epicurean theory.[9]

The first men [...] did not know how to kindle a fire nor how to clothe their bodies in the products and hides of wild animals, but they inhabited the bush and forest and caves of the mountains and they hid their unwashed bodies in the brush, driven to avoid the whipping winds and the rain, nor were they able to look to a common good nor did they know to employ any customs or laws among themselves and whatever booty one obtained by chance, he learned to keep for himself and to live by himself.[10]

They had sex when the urge came upon them both with the willing and the unwilling and they lived at the mercy of the elements like brute beasts, in fear during the night, and they fought with clubs and stones, and were carried off, one by one, by beasts of prey. (At least they did not die in their thousands in battle.) It was only when men mastered clothing and fire and married and saw the children of their marriage that mankind first began to soften its hard life and to keep faith with one another.[11]

Aristotle had his own theory.[12] The first human unit was the family – in Greek the *oikos* – man, wife, slave or ox and land ruled by the man. The *oikos* expands naturally into a village with sons, daughters and grand-children, and the eldest man was the ruler. Villages then combine for security and self-sufficiency to form the first political unit, the *polis*, which has as its purpose to provide the good life to its citizens. Men have a natural drive to form a state, but they must also curb their other natural desires with justice. Justice is essential to the State. On this point all the theorists agreed.

The State eventually developed into its best form,[13] in which

> everyone fears everyone and man fears man and class fears class; then, since no one feels secure just in himself, the people and the powerful reach an agreement and from this was created [. . .] a kind of conjoined state. For nature is not the mother of justice nor is human will, but [the mother of justice is] weakness. Now of three possibilities – either to do an injury and not suffer an injury, or to both do an injury and suffer an injury, or neither – the best is the first, to act without punishment if you can, the second is neither to do or to suffer an injury, but the most miserable is to be acted upon by force and to suffer injury.

And that is the basis of the philosophers' explanation of the origin of war – the will to live in peace without injustice[14] – and that explanation of the origin of war brings us back to Homer. In the *Iliad* the Greeks conclude that they have suffered an injustice, they send envoys to the Trojans to seek redress and when they are refused they seek recompense in war. Once the war begins, envoys still might travel from one side to the other and, as heralds with sacred stature and protection, travel safely. Greek heralds announced the means by which the Trojans could end the war – pay an indemnity and return Helen – and the Trojans rejected the demands. Trojan envoys brought Paris' offer to fight a single combat with Menelaus to determine who would get Helen. The leaders, Agamemnon and Priam, swore oaths and Menelaus and Paris fought. Menelaus won the duel, but Hera and Athena subverted the agreement. Oaths have little power against the gods. Nonetheless, Hector debates within himself whether to try to reach an agreement to end the war, even as Achilles is approaching with the intention to kill him.

Even at that late hour, if the Greeks and Trojans had been able to reach an agreement to end the war, had sworn oaths and had kept them honestly, the result would have been 'friendship and obedience to oaths' (*philoteta* and *horkiapista*), not 'peace'. Peace would have been a consequence of the oaths and certainly a good thing, but not a thing sought in its own name. The two belligerents would not have said, 'Now we are at peace'. Rather they would have said, 'Now we are friends where before we were enemies'. Greeks recognised three categories of relationships between states: none, friendship and war.

As the *polis* developed more democratic institutions it established a legal process to declare war; in both Sparta and Athens the citizens met in assembly where magistrates attempted to persuade them to vote 'yes' or 'no' on war.[15] The declaration of war was thus political but, at the same time, it was also part of a religious process, an appeal to the gods to uphold a just cause.[16]

We attack and take revenge on those who seek to injure us, and we inflict as much punishment as is allowed by fairness and humanity[17] [...] but no war is a just war, unless the causes are stated and the complaint is lodged first.[18]

So far everyone might agree, but who discriminates the just from the unjust? A threatened party can appeal to an abstract justice upheld by the gods but, on the mundane level, with no ruling authority the victims have little recourse except to appeal to powerful allies, if they have them. States of equal power might agree to submit to arbitration, if they can agree on an arbitrator, and arbitration is often a part of a peace treaty, although the same difficulty exists: finding an arbitrator both parties trust.

Even the historian, as Thucydides makes clear, cannot easily answer the question of justice, given the complexities of the causes – in his case – of the Peloponnesian War. He defines three distinct types of causes that led to the war: the long term causes – the growth of Athenian power and the Spartans' fear of that power; the short term causes – the war between Corinth and Corcyra, the Megarian decree and the siege of Potidaea; and the immediate cause – the Theban attack on the Athenian ally, Plataea.

The Spartans did not believe that the war was inevitable. They offered proposals to settle enough of the issues to satisfy their allies and prevent a war. The Athenian leader, Pericles, used the technicalities of arbitration to extend the negotiations indefinitely while ostensibly agreeing to arbitrate as he continued the actions which were drawing the Spartans into war. The Spartans proposed several different courses of action the Athenians could take to prevent war: lift the siege of Potidaea or rescind the Megarian decree. (Pericles told the Spartan envoy that the people had passed the decree and there it was. The Spartan asked if he couldn't just 'turn the decree to the wall?')[19] The Athenians rejected all of these proposals. Nonetheless, the Spartans later concluded that they had committed an injustice by going to war, because they had refused arbitration (even though Pericles had set unacceptable terms for the arbitration).

The comic poet Aristophanes[20] has a simpler explanation of the cause of the war: in a parody of Herodotus some young drunken Athenians steal a prostitute from Megara, and in retaliation some Megarians steal two prostitutes from Aspasia's establishment, at which point 'Olympian Pericles' thundered and lightning-ed and brought war on the whole of Greece.

Socrates engages Alcibiades in a more sophisticated discussion of justice and the cause of wars.[21] He edges into the subject by asking Alcibiades to judge what is better or worse in music, gymnastics and food; Alcibiades can easily define what is 'better' in each case. Then Socrates asks him, 'And as regards the question of "better", how about war? How would you define what is better? Tell me its name'.

'I am completely at a loss,' Alcibiades says.

'Well then,' Socrates asks, 'when and under what circumstances should one go to war?'

Alcibiades doesn't know, but he can characterise the charges brought against the enemy, that (109b) they 'have cheated us or used force against us or robbed us of something'. And he continues that one certainly should not go to war against the just but, somehow, the enemy always proves to be unjust.

The *polis* was not the only entity in Greece that could declare war. The Delphic Amphictyony (the council of the neighbours of the oracle at Delphi) met regularly to oversee the shrine; if it decided that the sanctuary had been violated, it could impose sanctions and even declare a sacred war against the offending party. The primary violation was encroachment upon the sacred land. The violation of one's territory was an undeniable act which would justly precipitate a war. That is why, when the Messenian envoys asked the Spartan king who was leading his army into Messenia,

'Are you really going to lead your army against your brothers?'

He replied, 'No, I'm just going to walk through their territory to the land that is vacant'.[22]

Greeks could consider a peace treaty unbroken even if they found themselves on a battlefield opposed to the other signatory. Treaties defined a set number of years in which the former belligerents would not make war on each other. The terms for these treaties reflected their character – libations (*spondai*) with conditions (*synthekai*) and oaths (*horkoi*). So, during the peace of Nicias which ended the first phase of the Peloponnesian War, the Athenians joined their allies at Mantinea and fought a battle against the Spartans. At that point, the Spartans did not consider that the treaty had been broken but, when the Athenians raided Laconia, then the Spartans did conclude that the Athenians had violated the oaths of the peace of Nicias and that they were again at war with Athens.[23]

In the end, the question of justice and injustice was decided by the stronger. The Athenians considered that their empire was a just empire more because they were a great city than for any abstract moral reasons.[24] Later generations praised themselves because they had gone to war only to support their allies.[25] The Athenian general Nicias defended the empire by saying that the Athenians fought against the Persians for Greek freedom while their Greek subjects had joined the Persians to help enslave the

Athenians. Nonetheless, though the Athenians professed the justice of their empire,[26] their leaders, like Cleon and Alcibiades, formulated the most ruthless policy – executing thousands of 'rebels' and wiping out Mitylene, Melos and cities in Chalcidice – and they justified the most brutal actions in the name of the realities of empire. Athens' most infamous act of brutality was the siege and destruction of Melos. In a debate with the Melians, the Athenians stated bluntly that they would do what they deemed to be in their own self-interest because they were strong enough to do what they wanted. They rejected the Melians' appeal to justice.

The Spartans defeated the Athenians and imposed an empire even more brutal than the Athenian, but they, in turn, were defeated, Greece was collectively weaker and some thoughtful men began to advocate for universal justice, freedom and peace. The Athenian rhetorician Isocrates (influential in 'modern' times)[27] presented an essay on justice, supposedly a speech by the Spartan king Archidamus.

> I am told to do what is expedient, but what is more expedient, than to do justice? Is not a man destroyed by injustice, but saved by justice? Do not nations, in the end, win wars because their cause is just? Did we not establish our system of law to make us just?[28]

Greeks sought a common peace (*koine eirene*) in which all would participate and cooperate to punish the few transgressors, but such a 'common peace' only worked when it was imposed by a power strong enough to enforce it. Philip, king of the Macedonians, for instance, founded a new League of Corinth and enforced a common peace extending to all the League's members. This peace did not outlive Philip and his son Alexander.

No general Greek work on the theory and ethics of war is extant, although the philosophical schools discussed them and different authors reflect these discussions. Polybius, for instance, writes,

> To destroy the enemy's forts, harbours, cities, soldiers, ships, and crops, and all the other such, through which you weaken the enemy, the

laws of war necessitate these acts and it is just to do so, but when you are neither going to strengthen your own cause, nor weaken the enemy by damaging shrines, statues, and all such work, you might say it is the work of an unbalanced mind.[29]

The first extant work to treat the theory and ethics of war is *de officiis* by the Roman orator Cicero. This work is based on earlier Greek works, to a large extent the work of two philosophers, Panaetius of Rhodes and Carneades (who had delivered two lectures in Rome; on one day supporting justice in war, on the other knocking it down and on both days being utterly convincing). Panaetius and Carneades, of course, reflected earlier philosophers. Cicero summarises the theories of these philosophers and adds to them Roman practices which, he affirms, were far superior to the Greek (specifically in ensuring justice in initiating and prosecuting wars).

Cicero distinguishes the two main areas of moral discussion about war; the *jus ad bellum*, the necessity to have a just cause for going to war, and the *jus in bello*, the just waging of war. These two issues are as alive today as they were then.

After Cicero sums up Greek theories of war, he adds to them Roman religious practices which, when conducted properly, ensure that every Roman war will be a just war (*bellum justum*).[30]

The *fetiales*, the priests in charge of war, determined if there was a just cause for war and prohibited the Romans from entering upon an unjust war. They oversaw the processes of war (and also determined if the Romans, or some Romans, had committed a wrong in violation of their treaties). If they determined that a wrong had been committed the *fetial* priest, in full ceremonial garments, travelled to the border of the offending state, proclaimed his purpose at the border and swore to its truth. Then he crossed the border, repeated his claim and oath to the first person he met, repeated the claim and oath to the gate keeper of the offending city, entered the city and went to the forum where he repeated his claim and oath to the magistrates and then conferred with them. If they agreed to give recompense he left 'as a friend', but if they needed to confer he granted them ten days, and he would grant two additional ten-day periods when needed. If, at the end of 30 days, they had not agreed – or if they had refused outright – he would return to the Roman Senate and announce that Rome had the right to go to war.

The Romans – to give an example – had made a treaty with the city of Tarentum that they would never sail into the Gulf of Tarentum but, decades later, on their way to put down pirates in the Adriatic and help Greek cities there, with no hostile intent, they brought their fleet into the gulf and the Tarentines attacked them. The Roman Senate concluded that they had a legitimate grievance and they sent a delegation to demand redress, but the envoys arrived in Tarentum while the citizens were celebrating a festival; the drunken crowd gathered and jeered at the Romans and one member of the crowd defecated in his hand and threw it on a Roman senator. The senator said, 'You will wash this garment clean with your blood', and the envoys withdrew.[31] (The Tarentines sobered up and asked Pyrrhus, the king of Epirus, to come to their aid.) The Roman envoys reported to the Senate that their demands had been rejected and the Senate decided that there was cause for war and initiated the religious rites necessary for prosecuting a just war (*bellum justum*); they sent heralds to cast a spear into Tarentine territory and to inform three individuals that war existed between the Romans and the Tarentines.

Because the Romans followed procedure, both civil and religious, Cicero, referring to the *fetial* law, could say to the Senate,

> Is it not true, conscript fathers, that the gods themselves love us? [...] By our piety and our religion and by this one single wisdom, given by the power of the gods, we have seen how to rule and to govern, and so we dominate all races and nations.[32]

Cicero identifies two valid reasons for war – retaliation and self-defence – but even so, a war is not a just war unless it has been declared, unless it has been announced to the enemy and unless the enemy has been given a chance to make reparation.[33]

In Cicero's own day the ritual was still performed (religiously), but the reality had changed. The Roman system of the late Republic at its most basic gave a commander an army, an area of operations (province) and a free hand. Romans competed for those offices which included a military command and then competed for a province in which, or from which, they could carry out a campaign to add territory to the Roman Empire and money and prestige to themselves.

Plutarch, in his life of Julius Caesar, writes that the Romans found in Gaul 3 million Gauls of whom they killed 1 million, enslaved 1 million and 'pacified' 1 million.[34] Caesar's conquest began with the legitimate defence of Roman territory. The Helvetians had attacked the Romans and the Romans had the perfect right to defend themselves. Caesar's pursuit of the Helvetians was not without justification, both as an active defence and as retaliation, and he could justify acceding to a request from his Gallic allies to help them defend themselves from a German invasion – the long term interests of Rome were to prevent Germans from dominating Gaul – but his decision to go into winter quarters in Gaul proves to us, as it did to the Gauls, that the Romans had come to stay. Then, after the first winter, the northern Gauls, the Belgae, 'conspired' against Rome – as Caesar and the Romans saw it – and Caesar was justified in defending himself.

Cicero, however, looked away from his own day back to a time of simplicity, grandeur and patriotism, when 'fairness in war' was 'prescribed by the most sacred *fetial* law of the Roman people'.[35]

> Those enemies, even with our army surrounding them, even if the ram is striking their walls, even then, justice is so strong with us, if they trust in the good will of our generals we receive them into our good faith, and, according to the customs of our ancestors, become their patrons.

A Roman war concluded when the enemy was destroyed or was ready to make an unconditional surrender (*deditio*) without knowing what would be done with them; whether they would be accepted as friends and allies of the Roman people or slaughtered or sold into slavery. Victory was presented to the Roman people in the form of a triumph celebrating the prowess of the commander.

> For the individual commanders the area they conquered, as well as adding territory to the Roman Empire, also gave them clients. That is, the Roman commanders became the patrons of the territory and the people they conquered.[36]

In theory, the bond between patron and client was like the bond between father and family (a Roman father, that is, with the power of life and death). The conquered people could call upon their patron for protection, though in practice the benefits of the conquest accrued largely to the patron (and his army).

Nonetheless, Cicero could say, 'Our rule of the world could more fairly be called a patrimony rather than an empire'.[37] Our equivalent would be something like, 'a big happy family with Father Rome at the head'.

Still, there is a measure of truth in what Cicero says, because the Romans co-opted the conquered ruling class (those who survived the war) and in time granted them Roman citizenship, binding them securely to Rome. Romans justified their wars because the Romans brought benefits to the conquered, including protection from attack. 'For the most part your ancestors waged great and serious wars for the safety of our allies and friends'.[38]

In short, the Romans are just, they bring peace, they defend their allies and, if anyone needs more justification, well, they have a divine fate granting them the right to rule.

Caesar, Augustus and their successors believed no less and conducted wars on much the same theory as wars had been conducted since republican times, that is, until Constantine (r. 306–37) became the first Christian emperor. As Christian and emperor, he was both head of the Empire with the right to make war and, as God's appointed representative, head of the

Church with the right to require all Christians except clergy to serve in the army. Under Constantine, leaders of the Christian church had to come to terms with a Church tied, for the first time, to imperial power; Christian thinkers had no easy task in reconciling the exigencies of empire with the New Testament and so they drew more on the Old Testament to develop a coherent view.

Ambrose (339–97), the Bishop of Milan, adopted the position that, while in Christian doctrine the defence of oneself at the expense of the life of another is not justified, the defence of others, a companion for instance, is not only allowable but required by a sense of Christian duty and, therefore, by extension, the defence of the empire is justified even to the extent of taking the lives of the attackers.[39] Nonetheless, in a reflection on Plato *Laws* (quoted above), Ambrose advised Christians that their first duty is to conquer the enemy within themselves.[40]

St Augustine (354–430) believed in original sin, that man is born corrupt and only a strong temporal order can keep him from exercising the worst defects of a sinful character. The temporal order, then, must be upheld by Christians and, indeed, defended from outside (barbarian) invasion. Defensive war is justified but so, too, he maintained, were the earlier wars of the Republic which spread Roman government and peace to other nations, even though, he wondered, at what cost did the empire bring universal peace? St. Augustine, however, condemned the Roman belief that they were just and all their neighbours were unjust; even if the Romans were correct, they would have been better off to have cultivated good neighbours and lived together in peace. War should be waged only to punish wrongdoing, as a father punishes his son, and vengeance should stop with victory and then the victor should convert the defeated. Unfortunately Augustine lived in a violent age and he, and plenty of others, sought peace and security in vain as Vandals invaded North Africa and Goths sacked Rome.[41]

In the east the Byzantine emperor continued to use his authority to summon Christians to defend his realm, but in the west the empire was torn apart, the emperor disappeared and Church was separated from temporal powers.

The first western scholars, who in the twelfth century re-founded the study of the theory of war from which modern theories derive, all studied the same Roman authors, but they divided themselves into two groups: one group (the Ciceronians) looked back primarily to the Roman orators, while the second group (the Tacitists) looked back to the religious–philosophical–juridical writings of the Roman Empire. The two groups largely agreed on questions of *jus in bello*, but split on the justification for going to war (*jus ad bellum*).

Gratian, a twelfth-century jurist and monk, who compiled a collection of canon law which was still consulted as late as 1917, declared as a basic principle that a war must be just and must be declared.[42] Thomas Aquinas (1225–74) set forth three requirements for a just war:[43]

1. There must be a right cause – that is, one must either have suffered an injury or be attempting to recover property.
2. There must be right intention – *jus in bello* – which recognised the existence of combatants and noncombatants.
3. There must be a proper authority.

Aquinas considered the duly constituted authorities – those with the right to declare war – to be the Holy Roman Empire and the Pope (particularly with regard to the Crusades), but the right of self-defence needed no authority. Theorists in the later Middle Ages redefined 'proper authority' to reside in princes.

By the early Renaissance – the early fifteenth century – leading men in the Italian city-states, particularly the humanist leaders of Florence, were glorifying Rome,[44] its republican ideals as expressed by Cicero, its virtues and its justifications for war, all in the interests of the liberty of Florence and its domination of Tuscany.

Machiavelli (1469–1527) was the greatest of them all. His works, the *Art of War* and *The Prince* still seem fresh and pertinent today, if distressingly cynical. (Amazon.com offers more than 40 editions and, of those, one single edition is about 5500 on the bestseller list.) Machiavelli, in the

Art of War, relied heavily, but certainly not exclusively, on Frontinus for material, and mined Frontinus, and other classical authors, for examples for *The Prince*.[45] Perhaps his works seem modern because we can still accept, with some additions, the statement in 1590 of Sir Roger Williams, 'We must confesse Alexander, Caesar, Scipio, and Haniball, to be the worthiest and famoust warriors that ever were'.[46] Machiavelli concluded that a republic, with its different classes and the tension between the classes, created the strongest instrument for war – a citizen army.

Machiavelli advocated the study of history as a practical guide to stratagems and strategy – in the *Discourses* (3.10), for example, he advised the general to seek a decisive battle – and he recommended history also to guide the individual conduct of leaders, that is, the ruthless and amoral advance of personal politics. Machiavelli broke with the tradition of theological exposition and analysis of war and advocated war as a good thing, a theatre of virtue, as it were. In a concise summation in *The Prince* he writes, 'a just war is a necessary war',[47] that is, not that justice determines whether to go to war, but that the determination to go to war renders the war 'just'. His general philosophy today would be called *realpolitik*.

No other writer on war from this period is so well known as Machiavelli, but others, like Alberico Gentili and Francis Bacon, did write about war. Gentili in *de iure belli* (1588, rev 1598), categorised the various reasons for waging war which he derived from an analysis of the Roman emperors' justifications for war and conquest.[48] Their primary justification is preemption, based on fear (the very reason Thucydides gives for the Spartan declaration of war on Athens or, for a modern example, the invasion of Iraq to pre-empt the development and use of chemical, biological or nuclear weapons). Cicero said in a speech on Marc Antony:[49] 'Do not wait and then regret what you have suffered but be on your guard before you suffer, for it is a wretched thing, when you are in a position to prevent something dreadful, to ignore it and later repent'. Francis Bacon provides a succinct summation, 'A just fear [is] a just cause of a preventive war'.[50]

However, the justification of 'just fear' did not apply to the Europeans' wars with the native peoples of the New World. Theorists scrambled to justify (or condemn) these European wars of exploitation and conquest. One rationale, current in the mid-seventeenth century in Protestant and Calvinist communities, was drawn from the Old Testament: the 'chosen' people, that is, us, have no restriction upon their behaviour because they are waging a holy war; they reasoned that the Lord owns the Earth, we are his chosen people, and, QED, the Lord may give the Earth, or part thereof, to his chosen people, as He pleases.[51] In addition, they bolstered their argument with the Aristotelian view of natural slavery as reflected in a debate in 1550 in Valladolid, Spain, on the nature of native Americans, which concluded to the Europeans' advantage.

On the other hand, in the early sixteenth century, Erasmus of Rotterdam (1466–1536), humanist and priest, skirted heresy by suggesting that peace is better than war, that to be sure, there may be just wars, but they are so rare as to be negligible, and hard to define, because everyone thinks he is just and the others are unjust. His views form a kind of conclusion to Renaissance thought ... that human communities are morally equal and that all have a right to justice *ad bellum* and *in bello*.[52]

Hugo Grotius (1583–1645) is the seminal figure in the theory of war. The most prominent writer today on the ethics of war, Michael Walzer, in a letter to the *New York Times* referring to the article, 'How to Halt the Butchery in Syria', wrote,

Hugo Grotius was among the founders of international law. He wrote that when a state undertakes mass killings of its own citizens, it is not only the right but also the duty of surrounding nations to intercede [...] International law has developed in line with the proposition advanced by Grotius.[53]

Grotius studied, systemised and summed up thought before him, and his work became the basis for all subsequent discussion. Grotius' views were developed from a thorough mastery of the ancient sources, subsequent discussions and a background of Dutch expansion and aggression. (In his first chapter 'On War and Right', pp. 3–13, he cites Cicero, Aristotle, Seneca,

Euripides, Florentinus, Paulus, the *Septuagint*, Ulpian, Epictetus Arrian, Hesiod, Plutarch, Lactantius, Polybius, Heraclitus, Quintilian, Porphyry and Andronicus, to name a few.)

His method was to explore a question – for example, the just war – by analysing ancient sources including the Bible and church fathers, reconciling their differences, applying his own reasoning and reaching a conclusion.[54] For instance, the justifications for war are self-defence, recovery of property or debt, or punishment of offences. The claim of self-defence is justified only against an aggressor – an aggressor can never claim self-defence – nor can self-defence be claimed for an attack made on another power just because it is growing more powerful. He concludes with a thorough discussion of the rights of property and the types of property, contracts, promises, agents, oaths and treaties, and asks the pertinent question: What if both sides claim they have justice on their side?[55]

Grotius had to formulate a new theory for a new kind of war in his own time, a war not in defence of his own United Provinces, or even in the interests of defence, but of expansion and booty. Moreover, no clear governing body was making the decisions of war and peace.[56] Grotius found an analogy in the powers of a civil magistrate to use force – for the Roman magistrate the power of *coercitio*, which derives from the right of the head of the family – the *paterfamilias* – to use force against members of his own family. The magistrate's right of coercion against citizens does not derive exactly from the State, because the State only possesses its powers through the consent of its citizens. By the same reasoning the State does not have any inherent power to use force against another state, but rather the power, or right, to use force derives from the law of nature (or 'law of nations'). Grotius used Roman sources to validate these views.

Grotius enunciates two fundamental laws of nature – the right to defend oneself and (citing Cicero) the right to acquire the means of life. War is a part of nature – the bull has horns, the lion teeth and claws, and man a hand to wield a sword – and, therefore, has associated with it natural rights.[57] He adds two further laws: the right to defend other persons from attack and the right to defend the property of others.

To define the 'Rights of War' he cites Cicero's view that depriving another of what is rightfully his is repugnant. No society can exist which does not protect against unlawful seizure. He cites Seneca's view that members of society are like members of the body, in that they exist only as part of a collective whole, but Grotius distinguishes the right that an individual has to himself from the rights inherent in the superior position of some individuals in society to others (for example, master to slave) and, finally, of the state to the individual.[58]

Book II analyses the reasons for going to war (*jus ad bellum*) in detail with all permutations. Book III discusses what is lawful in war (*jus in bello*) and concludes that 'all things necessary to the end are lawful'.[59]

Considering that *De iure Belli ac Pacis* (1625) is about 400 years old and uses ancient sources as authorities in a way we would not today, it remains remarkably fresh because it discusses the very questions we discuss. For instance, are we justified in attacking another country because we believe it may be planning to attack us? (The aggressor may never make a legitimate claim of self-defence.) Grotius' reasoning is that the right to defend ourselves is absolute. We also have the right to defend what is ours and that includes, if we own land, the creatures that live on that land, whereas we do not have the right to intervene on land we do not own. The spirit of his work is this: we can, by examining ancient authorities and using our own powers of reason, arrive at rules for declaring and conducting war (*jus ad bellum* and *jus in bello*).

As for European aggression against native peoples, these peoples have no right to what they do not use; if they have land they do not farm, others may farm it or, if they have surplus resources, they must share.[60] This conclusion he derives from Cicero, Seneca and Plutarch – when it does not hurt us to give something to others who need it, we do a wrong not to share it. Taken to its extreme, Grotius' theories justified the European occupation of North America – Indians did not 'use' (that is, *farm*) the land, they could not claim ownership of the buffalo and they did not mine the silver of the Black Hills. These were not mere abstract theories – states

acted on their basis. The idea that land not owned could be freely occupied was cited even to justify some wars between Europeans.

The issues argued by ancient theorists and developed by Grotius are still
the subjects of debate and discussion today. Perhaps no question has been
as vexed, and given rise to such heat, as the question of the origins of war
and basic human nature. Is mankind predisposed to war or have other factors
driven mankind to engage in warfare?

Grotius believed that war was natural and Thomas Hobbes (1588–
1679) in *Leviathan* agreed with him. In a state of nature before cities,
before kings, before communities, before a time when there was 'a common
power to keep them all in awe, they are in that condition which is called
war; and such a war as is of every man against every man'.[61] We could call
these the Hesiodic, or Stoic, view; that strife is a natural part of human
nature and must be kept in check by justice.

Three philosophers born in the same year, Baruch Spinoza (1632–77),
Samuel von Pufendorf (1632–94) and John Locke (1632–1704) addressed
exactly this subject.

Spinoza, in *Tractatus Politicus* (1677), argued that a state with good laws,
reason and individual freedom could secure the rights of men and society,
and thus secure peace. The best state, therefore, is a state where men live
together in harmony under good laws. He cites as an example of harmony
that it was 'regarded as a remarkable virtue in Hannibal that there was
never a mutiny in his army'.[62]

Locke postulated an original state of nature without a sovereign and
(unlike Hobbes) without war. This original state of nature established the
'law of nature'. The law of nature, then, makes certain demands on men in
societies that they live together in peace and that the sovereign authority,
even a king, be based fundamentally on the consent of the people. Society,
then, exists, or should exist, to preserve the rights of men.

Von Pufendorf believed in a natural law derived from God, which
commanded men to be sociable and to look to the interests of others but,
unfortunately, men are imperfect (because of the fall) and tend towards

self-interest more than they should, so that they need the justice that states provide. This natural law also applied to states which, like people, should be sociable towards each other and try to live in harmony. (Unfortunately, no supra-society exists to furnish international justice.)

Out of these discussions and counter-arguments grew the modern concept of natural law, articulated by Christian von Wolff (1679–1754) as the 'law of nations', which should determine relations between states.

Jean-Jacques Rousseau (1712–78) was the most articulate champion of the theory that man was a gentle creature corrupted by the State. He rejected the notion that the natural condition of man was one of vicious self-interest, but rather that it was a condition of bliss destroyed by the creation of society and the State. It is civilisation – and the State – that has given rise to conflict and to war. 'War is [...] not a relationship between one man and another, but a relationship between one state and another, in which individuals are enemies only by accident.'[63] A man alone in nature whose needs are satisfied has no requirement for more, but in a state 'surplus awakens greed'.[64] The State's power is relative, it fears stronger neighbours, it desires to acquire more land and to expand and can expand only at the expense of its neighbours, and it constantly seeks a security it can never attain. 'War consists in the constant, reflective, and manifest will to destroy one's enemy'.[65]

He sums his views up by relating a vision that he had of himself: he is reading and agreeing with the earlier authors on the benefits of civilisation and then he steps outside his study to find 'an enraged mob [...] whose blood and tears the rich drink in peace'.[66] Rousseau advocated an idea, current in his time, of a supranational state, a confederation of all states, which would have the power to curb ambitious men and bring universal and permanent peace.

Must we conclude, then, that, without a higher authority, war is inevitable?

Immanuel Kant (1724–1804) set forth a number of principles which, if followed, would ensure a universal peace: peace must be made without reservation; no state may acquire another state; no state may have a standing army; no state may have a national debt (whereby it may support a large army); no state shall interfere in the affairs of another state; and, finally, if states are at war they will conduct themselves so that they do not create a permanent enmity.[67] He promoted republican (democratic) governments because, he believed, they will not wage war on each other, whereas when one individual (or a few) has the power to make war, they do make war. Nonetheless, despite his opposition to war, he did affirm that there still remains an overriding moral imperative which requires us to act in certain circumstances.

In contrast, G. W. F. Hegel (1770–1831) insisted on the distinctiveness of the State, not just as a collection of individuals, but as something higher in a kind of evolution of the human condition in which the individual is willing to sacrifice himself for the State. War is a necessary part of history. Karl Marx (1818–83) and Friedrich Engels (1820–95) rejected the idea that a world divided into nation-states is the culmination of the history of mankind; rather it is a stage through which human beings must pass on their way to the great revolution which will bring the international and classless society . . . and the end of war.

Today the origin of war is more the subject of psychologists, anthropologists, primatologists and, for that matter, in 1961 one critically acclaimed playwright, Robert Ardrey. In *African Genesis* (the first popular work to postulate our less than peaceful origins) Ardrey states his simple thesis – we are the descendants of killer apes.[68] This thesis was ridiculed at the time and, indeed, one anthropologist in the 1960s found his career threatened because of his description of violence in an Amazonian society[69] but, since then, scientists have sought the explanation of war in natural animal aggressiveness.[70] Psychologists identify frustration as the motive for an act of aggression which results in individual attacks and attacks of society upon society. Anthropologists used to identify the ancestor of man as a gentle, vegetable-eating primate, and scholars stuck to their hypothesis of the gentle, but corrupted, human primate, until Jane Goodall's report that chimpanzees wage war. Her report was vehemently rejected at first, because it contradicted the deeply held conviction that man was the only creature that waged war and that man, therefore, could not be predisposed to war.[71] The evidence was dismissed as inconclusive until a researcher actually followed chimpanzees in the wild.[72]

The studies of chimpanzees in the wild suggest that war is a function of community, certainly the most primitive community imaginable, but is 'natural' or 'innate', if not inevitable. To go beyond that, to suggest, like a recent book title – *War is the Force That Gives Us Meaning* – that not only are we disposed towards war but we like it is, to say the least, disturbing. However, if humans are predisposed to war, then the definition of *jus ad bellum* becomes critical to the relations of nations and, indeed, to our own wellbeing.

The first and most important question is, who has the right to declare war? The ready answer was, the duly constituted authorities. Samuel von Pufendorf maintained, in a stable system of states, that states, unlike the individual, have the moral right to declare war. That is, that the duly constituted authority is the State. As to the causes of war, he insists that the primary, and only certain, justification for going to war is self-defence. Self-defence is an absolute right.

Hobbes had already accepted not only the right of self-defence but the universal acknowledgement of that right – we might attack you for the clearest and most righteous reasons, and you might be the wickedest people on the face of the earth but, even so, we accept your right to defend yourself. John Locke went further by asserting the right, if necessary, to defend oneself by attacking and even conquering another. (Nonetheless, even in conquest, the conqueror should act justly towards the conquered and preserve their lives and property.) Of course, the devil is in the detail.

Samuel von Pufendorf asserted the moral right of states to prosecute wars and, in addition, although states should prefer to conduct war under a declaration of war and against states which have committed acts of war, they are not forbidden to wage war without a declaration against states which harbour or abet evil-doers, even if those states do not have a formal policy of support for the evil-doers. (This is the doctrine behind the 'war on terror' or actions against pirates.)[73]

Philosophers pretty well dismissed the validity of any claim of a 'just' war because all sides claim that justice is with them. Emer De Vattel (1714–67) concluded that one cannot choose between the causes promoted by the several states to decide if one was just and another not. And, in fact, the justice of a cause is somewhat immaterial in the face of the prosecution of the war (the *jus in bello*). That being so, the question is, in what circumstances, except for self-defence, can war be justified? How far can self-defence be stretched? Does it extend to pre-emptive strikes?[74]

The political thinker Baron de Montesquieu (1689–1755) asserted – in reaction to von Pufendorf's praise of a stable balance of power – that the system of armed states, particularly as each mobilised its resources, created a danger which could be controlled only by the agreements and cooperation of liberal states. As the State promotes the rights and prosperity of its citizens, the citizens merge together and, in a way, form a new entity with the rights, not only of self-defence against invasion, but of engaging in a pre-emptive defence.[75]

De Vattel posed the question, must we stand by and let a neighbour grow strong and wait until it attacks us, before we go to war? Must we, in short, stand by, perhaps, until we are no longer able to defend ourselves? His answer was no – if the opponent has given evidence of ill will and has committed unjust acts, we need not wait to defend ourselves and, furthermore, the right of self-defence extends to a situation in which the enemy does not pay us our just due. (In the Japanese decision to go to war against Britain and the United States Hideki Tojo said, 'As to what our moral basis for going to war should be, there is some merit in making it clear that Great Britain and the US represent a strong threat to Japan's self-preservation.')[76]

Theorists and political leaders reacted to each other, the latter seeking justification for acts already committed, the former, using Greek and Roman writers – in particular, Cicero – furnishing a moral structure for the circumstances of their own time. If, for instance, the only clear justification of waging war is self-defence, even if self-defence is extended to pre-emption, how can the conquest and exploitation of the Americas, India and Africa be justified?

John Stuart Mill (1806–73) in 'A Few Words on Non-Intervention' addresses just that question. In such a case – the attack by a civilised nation upon 'barbarians' – the civilised nation has a moral obligation to civilise the barbarians by ejecting tyrants and establishing a civilised nation. (At the heart of his argument is the question whether Gaul, for instance, would have been better off if it had never been conquered by Rome. His answer is no.) His argument justified colonisation.[77]

However, in the case of sovereign nations, the question was, under what circumstances and conditions should a nation interfere in the affairs of another nation? As so many others had, Mill accepts self-defence as an incontestable right, but what are the criteria for intervention, when self-defence is not the issue or, to the contrary, what are the criteria for refraining from intervening? It is a moral wrong for one nation to overthrow another government, unless it is prepared to set up a new (and better) government in its place, a government comprising people who were fighting for their freedom against a repressive government. In short, intervention has certain moral requirements and it should also have prudent requirements, that it truly is in our interests, that it can succeed and that war to achieve the results we want is not worse than the present situation.

Mill applied this reasoning to the specific case whether Great Britain should aid the South in the American Civil War. He concluded that Great Britain should not intervene, even though in general he supported insurrections fought for liberty, because, in this case, the institution of slavery was so great a wrong that supporting the South would involve the British in that same great moral wrong. Sometimes war is necessary. Some causes are worth fighting for. 'As long as justice and injustice have not terminated their ever-renewing fight for ascendancy in the affairs of mankind, human beings must be willing, when need is, to do battle for the one against the other'.[78]

The philosophers who believed in the just war – von Pufendorf and Locke, for example – also asserted that the just must adhere to judgements of right and wrong when fighting even against the unjust, that is, to preserve life and property and not to make permanent enemies out of the defeated. Hegel added that warring states should conduct themselves according to certain rules, not, however, rules based on some moral code, but those which have developed out of practice. This code, which they called 'natural law', was redefined by Christian von Wolff (1679–1754) to form the modern concept of the 'law of nations'. The law of nations is supposed to be the basis of the relations between states.

The law of nations, according to von Wolff, defined and delineated the limits of military action: that it should be limited to just what is necessary to defeat the enemy and that it should not involve the civilian population. Moreover, it establishes that those whose cause is just have no more right to violate the 'necessities of war' than do those whose cause is unjust and, further, as far as the perception of justice goes, since every state believes that its cause is just, it cannot stand as a judge of another state. For that reason, he rejects wars fought because the enemy hold different religious views.

Although a state has a limited right of reprisal, if all other means of redress have been exhausted, still the reprisals have limits, regardless of what the enemy has done. For example, to encourage one's soldiers to commit rape is wrong regardless of whether the enemy soldiers have engaged in rape, even if the enemy encouraged it as a matter of policy. In addition, as soon as an enemy is captured, he can no longer be treated as an enemy (since he is totally in the power of the captor and can no longer wage war).

Emer De Vattel (1714–67) summed up the law of nations in a sentence: all parties are required to adhere to certain rules; only that conduct is permissible in war which is necessary to achieving victory; all else – that which is not necessary – is not permissible.[79]

In practical terms governments struggled with the application of these theories. In the American Revolution, General Washington insisted on a close adherence to the law of nations (as expressed by Vattel) which held that soldiers would fight soldiers while respecting the persons and property of civilians. The British were less particular, first, because they did not recognise the revolution as legitimate war, so that their opponents, military and civilians, from top to bottom, were traitors and, second, because their self-interest was not involved in upholding the 'law' whereas, as

Washington pointed out, the revolutionary combatants would have to live in the country they had fought over.[80] In sum, much of law [...] is made up of what can be 'plausibly argued and forcibly maintained'.[81]

Not everyone agreed in the validity of the law of nations. Most famously, Carl von Clausewitz (1780–1831), a veteran and student of the Napoleonic Wars, maintained in *On War* (1832, published posthumously) that war's only rule is victory. 'Attached to force are certain self-imposed, imperceptible limitations hardly worth mentioning, known as international law and custom.'[82] 'War is nothing but a duel on a larger scale'. He advocates the maximum use of force (necessary to win the war) and rejects kindness and moderation as having no place in war but, rather, weakening the side that attempts to be moderate. War grows out of the politics of a country and is a political act. Therefore, war is merely the continuation of policy by other means.[83] 'War is thus an act of force to compel our enemy to do our will.' *On War* became enormously influential. It was read by military leaders and it created an attitude towards war which its adherents thought of as 'realistic' as opposed to the 'liberal' advocates of a strict adherence to the law of nations. (Von Clausewitz has been slightly misinterpreted – he advocated a short, intense, no-holds-barred war which would get the job done quickly and with less damage to the combatants than a long war lengthened by moral constraints.)

Nonetheless, there was a growing sense that soldiers should conduct themselves in a certain way. During the American Civil War Lincoln gave Francis Lieber (1800–72) the task of establishing military rules of conduct for the Union forces. Lieber had served in the Napoleonic Wars in the Prussian army, had been severely wounded and left for dead on the battlefield, but survived and, through a series of adventures, wound up teaching in South Carolina. He had three sons; one fought for the Confederacy and the other two for the Union. One son was severely wounded in the Union army at the battle of Fort Donelson. Lieber rather followed Hegel, and his own experience, to write that war brought out the best in men; 'energy and independence of thought, elevation and firmness of character, intensity of action'.[84] The rules he formulated, issued in 1863, were intended to codify custom, practice, theory, and law in concrete form for commanders and soldiers in the field. They were to define *jus in bello* and covered a multiplicity of subjects including martial law, the rights of personal and public property, retaliation, protection of persons, religion, art, punishment of crimes against the hostile population, prisoners of war, booty, partisans, spies and flags of truce.

When, for example an invading army imposes martial law on the territory it occupies, it has complete authority but, nonetheless, it must still adhere to the principles of 'justice, honour and humanity'.[85] Article 15 addresses the killing of the enemy and the destruction of property and allows all actions which are designed to weaken the enemy and lead to victory, but prohibits cruelty. Soldiers, the code states, are 'moral beings responsible to one another and to God'. Lieber states, as a principle, in Article 29 that between nations peace is the normal condition and war has as its ultimate object the restoration of peace. Articles 56 and 80 treat of prisoners of war: prisoners of war may not be treated as public enemies once captured and may not be punished. Prisoners should not give information about their own armies and should not be forced by torture to give such information

A summation of nineteenth-century thinking can be found in the 1868 Declaration of St Petersburg:[86]

The progress of civilisation should have the effect of alleviating as much as possible the calamities of war.

The only legitimate object which states should endeavour to accomplish during war is to weaken the military force of the enemy.

For this purpose, it is sufficient to disable the greatest possible number of men.

This object would be exceeded by the employment of arms which uselessly aggravate the sufferings of disabled men, or render their death inevitable.

The employment of such arms would, therefore, be contrary to the laws of humanity.

For the United States the Civil War was a traumatic event which changed American military leaders' attitudes towards war, even though those who had not participated believed in the romance of it. William Tecumseh Sherman, in a speech in Columbus, Ohio, said, 'There is many a boy here today who looks on war as all glory, but, boys, it is all hell.'[87]

More Americans were killed in the Civil War than in all other American wars combined – the effects of artillery and the rifle made the cost of a massed frontal assault so great that military men looked for another way to fight – but what was true for Americans was ignored by the military of Europe (except for the German study of the Union's employment of rail) until the catastrophic losses of World War I convinced them that a frontal attack upon a prepared position by unsupported infantry was too costly to sustain. Consequently, twentieth century military theorists sought both to reinvent tactics and also to find a way to limit war if they could not altogether prevent it. The use of poison gas had been so devastating that its future use was prohibited, and to the present day no major military force has used it. The effectiveness of this prohibition is cited as proof that extraordinarily vicious weapons can be outlawed successfully – although nations still stockpile poison gas to use in retaliation, if necessary.

The victors of the 'war to end all wars', ignoring the sage advice of Samuel von Pufendorf and Woodrow Wilson, created the conditions for World War II. World War II was no less terrible on the front lines than World War I had been, but it was even more terrible for civilians, who were targeted by both sides in the war. The Germans bombed London in the expectation that the bombing would bring Britain to its knees. The British responded and carried out a systematic campaign against civilian targets long after such a campaign was proven futile. The American commander in England, General Carl Spaatz, protested the terror campaign against German civilians (more for tactical than moral reasons – as Eisenhower said, 'Let's for God's sakes, keep our eyes on the ball and use some sense'),[88] but then the American command conducted just such a campaign against Japan. The Japanese, likewise, had targeted civilians in China.

In February 1945 the Allies (principally the British) bombed Dresden.

The bombing destroyed the city and killed more than 25,000 civilians. Churchill called the attack an 'act of terror and wanton destruction'.[89] On 9 March 1945, American B-29 bombers attacked Tokyo with a combination of incendiary (napalm), high explosive and fragmentation bombs. The raid killed over 87,000 people and effectively destroyed Tokyo. US pilots were told, 'There are no civilians in Japan'.[90]

The ultimate decision on the targeting of civilians was the decision to use the atomic bomb against Japan. Some scientists felt general moral qualms – although they did not fully understand the effects of radiation, nonetheless they recognised that this weapon was different from all other weapons used in this war and in all previous wars. The prevailing opinion, however, can be summed up by Curtis LeMay's remarks, 'We just weren't bothered about the morality of the question; if we could shorten the war, we wanted to shorten it'.[91]

The Western Allies believed – and we still believe – that the war against the Axis was a just war, first, because the Allies were attacked and forced to defend themselves and, second, because they were fighting evil regimes. A British pilot named Tim Vigors said of killing the enemy, 'The way I saw it then was, "Poor son of a bitch. He was probably a nice guy and we would probably have got on well had we met. But he was on the wrong side. He shouldn't have signed up with that bastard Hitler."'[92] Such reflections reveal the acknowledgement that the enemy were human beings and yet, with all the discussions over the centuries of the necessities of *jus in bello*, targeting of civilians had become military doctrine and remained military doctrine in the nuclear age.

After the war the Allies began war-crimes trials at Nuremberg. The charges grew out of, first, the *jus ad bellum*; that neither the Germans nor the Japanese had had legitimate reasons for making war, that they had, in effect, waged aggressive war. Secondly, the tribunal concentrated on *jus in bello*; the atrocities committed during the war. While some questioned an *ex post facto* trial, in truth the conduct of powers, *ad* and *in*, had been discussed for 2,000 years and more, and the limits of conduct were firmly established. What was revealed at Nuremberg spoke for itself.

The more pressing issue was to prevent the next war. The Allies agreed to create an international body to arbitrate international disputes: the United Nations. They hoped that civilised nations – with the horrible example of the two world wars behind them – could establish an international law code, or code of conduct, which would enable nations to settle disputes without war and, finally, to be able to live in peace with each other.

Some believed, if wars now fell outside international law, as Cicero acknowledged, 'the laws fall silent amid arms'[93]; if so, how could there be talk of 'just' war? The United Nations tried to give a partial answer to those questions in Article 2 of its Charter: 'the first use of armed force by a State in contravention of the Charter shall constitute *prima facie* evidence of an act of aggression' and, therefore, the one attacked may, with justice, wage war and others may go to its defence. All states have the inherent right of self-defence (that is, that self-defence is not a war crime regardless of the reasons one must defend oneself). On the other hand, if we agree that the shedding of human blood is immoral, then shouldn't we all be pacifists? And yet, if we take so rigid a stance, won't we lose all control over war and the waging of war? Control is particularly important at this time when we seem to have come to an agreement that there is no difference between soldier and civilian.

The terror bombing of cities in World War II was not necessary, did not contribute to the end of the war and was immoral, but seems to have become established practice and, indeed, an important element in the strategy for nuclear war. Even if we agree that the deliberate targeting of the innocent is wrong – although the collateral damage to the civilian population while attacking legitimate targets, a regrettable consequence to be sure, is not wrong in the context of a just war – nonetheless, a nuclear exchange, by its nature, would have a devastating effect upon civilians. The best that modern theorists could do was to suggest that we accept a convention, like desert people fighting each other but not poisoning the wells, to limit the weapons we use and to redefine what we mean by *jus in bello*.

In general, modern theorists concluded what other theorists had concluded centuries before, that combatant and noncombatant should be treated differently, that the states should conduct themselves in a moral fashion and that a just war should conclude in a just peace.

The best modern summary, analysis and explication of the issues of war is Michael Walzer's (b. 1935), *Just and Unjust Wars*. The author is recognised as one of the most influential writers on this subject in modern times. In his preface he writes, as a college student preparing to protest the war in Vietnam, 'we found a moral doctrine ready at hand ...' and a vocabulary. He consciously chose a title for his book which reflected the arguments of Cicero and St Augustine. His purpose, enunciated in his preface, is not to argue an abstract moral philosophy, but rather to investigate historical examples and to analyse each to arrive at specific conclusions and from these conclusions to reach a general moral code of conduct based on actual human behaviour in war.

Michael Walzer asks the question, are wars so horrible, that it is pointless to seek rules by which to conduct war; in short, is *jus in bello* a fantasy? In a typical example of his reasoning he discusses terrorists. We – in the afflicted society – judge them to be murderers and prosecute them for murder when they are caught and yet we make moral judgements about them, depending upon their targets. If they target political or military leaders opposed to their cause, and avoid attacking civilians, even so far as to call off an attack when civilians would be casualties, we judge them in moral terms differently than we judge those who indiscriminately kill. And we also judge them according to our opinion of their target.

Walzer's conclusion is that morality can and should have a role in all war and warlike operations. In a specific example he discusses siege warfare. It is to the advantage of the besieged to rid themselves of everyone who does not contribute to the defence, as Vercingetorix did at the siege of Alesia; on the other hand, it is to the advantage of the besieger that as many people as possible remain in the besieged area to consume the resources of the besieged, as Caesar did by refusing to admit the population expelled by Vercingetorix.

Walzer begins his discussion of siege warfare with that very issue, the rights of the noncombatants caught up in the siege. He first discusses

the Roman siege of Jerusalem in AD 72. There the Roman commander
Titus kept the civilians within the city by ordering any person leaving
Jerusalem to be crucified. Walzer then compares Titus' policy with the
action of the German general in command at the siege of St Petersburg
(Leningrad) in World War II. The Soviets did not evacuate the civilian
population and the German commander ordered his artillery to fire on
refugees (in order to drive them back into the city). Walzer cites Grotius
(citing Maimonides) that the besieger should open an escape route for the
civilian population of the besieged city. If they have the opportunity to
leave but they remain, they have chosen to throw their lot in with the
military defenders and can expect to share their fate. The court at Nuremberg
found that the German general who ordered the artillery strikes on refugees
had not violated the international law of war. Walzer, however, uses the
issues of combatant and noncombatant in sieges to make a point about
the separation of the two in other situations. Walzer's conclusion is that
the besieged must be offered the chance to leave and the besieger must offer
safe conduct or, in a wider application wherever possible, in any war zone
noncombatants must be given the opportunity to leave the area of danger.

In the end, he follows a formulation of a code of conduct which is an
amalgamation of morality and realism, but tilted towards realism – the
military force is allowed to do what it must do to win a victory. When
General Bradley ordered the carpet bombing of an area to facilitate a surprise
assault, he knew that he would be causing the deaths of French civilians,
whom he could not warn because he would lose the element of surprise.
On this realist formulation, he was exactly within his rights. On the other
hand, once the British realised that the bombing of German cities was
unnecessary and that victory would be achieved without the bombing, they
should have stopped.

Walzer makes the point that often in a situation soldiers are going to
have to make a choice and often the situation does not allow reflection.
When we were in a firefight with the North Vietnamese and some panic-
stricken children ran into the crossfire, we stopped firing and the enemy
did not. The enemy did not violate international law and under this realist

formulation they were justified in continuing to shoot at us but, nonethe-less, following Walzer's formulation, both sides should have made the moral choice to allow the children time to get clear, assuming that such action would not give one side or the other an advantage.

Walzer emphasises the broader principle that a just war should conclude with a just and lasting peace, but such a peace will not be realised if the victor has used unjust methods – that is, atrocities and terrorism – to win the war. Therefore, the victor profits in the long run by adhering to a moral code of conduct.

In 1990 an American general, addressing the issue of the end of the Cold War, said to an audience at West Point, 'Frankly, gentlemen, I do not know what the future mission of the army will be'.[94] The new century soon provided a new mission; the countries of the world are still wrestling with the implications of the war on terror. In the case of the United States and the 9/11 attacks, the nations of the world generally agreed that the United States was justified in attacking the government of Afghanistan in that it had provided support and sanctuary to Al Qaida which had attacked the United States. The doctrine of retaliation and self-defence both were convincing arguments.

The case of Iraq was quite different. To persuade the United Nations, the United States had to present a persuasive argument that Iraq posed an immediate threat, that it had the means to carry out this threat and that it had been involved to some degree in the attack of 9/11. A convincing argument would have required the UN to concede that the United States had the rights of self-defence and retaliation against Iraq. The argument was not persuasive (and turned out to be wrong on all counts). In both cases, by the logic of John Stuart Mill, the United States assumed the moral duty to establish a fair and legitimate government in each country.

In a sense, theorists of war have held converse with each other for centuries, to dispute, edit and defend their theories. Cicero and St Augustine are still active participants in the discussion of justice and conduct in war, because they debated questions that go to the heart of human experience. The historical dialogue can be summed up as follows: war is justified, and only justified, to 'protect the innocent, to recover something wrongfully taken, to punish evil, and to defend against a wrongful attack in progress'.[95]

Until that day when all mankind shall live together in comity – or at least develop a non-violent means of settling quarrels – their discussion will continue. We should pay attention, not so much for any lofty moral or philosophical reason – though that is important in itself – but because paying attention to their advice may keep us from the consequences of bad decisions.

This truly is the legacy of ancient warfare.

CHAPTER V

WRITING WAR

The first literary descriptions of war concentrate on the deeds of the king.[1] Some of the kings kept journals (mostly lost) and had accounts of their exploits inscribed in temples and on monuments, but only rarely can a military historian reconstruct the tactics of a Near Eastern battle. For instance, one of the greatest and most significant wars fought in the ancient Near East was the defeat and destruction of the Assyrian kingdom, but the ancient accounts extend only to a couple of pages in a modern history.

In the earliest literate societies – Sumer, Akkad, Egypt (early third millennium) and China (mid-second millennium) – writing was the specialty of a rigorously trained scribal class. In the Near East the ruling elite limited the written accounts of their exploits to what they wanted others to know, but in China the literate class was more prolific, was considered particularly wise and, therefore, expert in military matters, and their military treatises were influential. The Chinese literate class considered war to be evil, a disharmony in the universe, and yet a subject which must be studied, because men express their own evil in war. They treated warfare as an intellectual exercise and the treatise as the instrument by which the ruler would attain military wisdom and success; they had little interest in tactics.[2]

In the ancient Near East the one big exception to a meagre literature is the Old Testament, which stands by itself for its full accounts of events, but which, nonetheless, gives short shrift to tactical details.

And it happened in those days that Israel [...] went out in battle against the Philistines [...]. And the Philistines drew their battle line up opposite Israel. At the very beginning of the battle, however, Israel turned its back to the Philistines and about 4,000 men were slain'.[3]

The Israelites brought the Ark of the Covenant into camp and the Philistines were afraid, but again ' the Philistines fought Israel and Israel was slaughtered and fled each one into his own home [...] and 30,000 Israelite foot were killed'.[4]

The description of the battle includes everything important to the author – that is, the revelation of God's will in the punishment of two sinners by the slaughter of Israel and the capture of the Ark – and it excludes everything extraneous – tactics, strategy, topography, the leaders' names ...

The most famous individual action in the Old Testament is the duel between David and Goliath.[5] Goliath of Gath was a giant more than nine feet tall and, in addition to his bronze helmet and bronze greaves, he wore a bronze breastplate which weighed 125 pounds, and he carried a bronze spear with an iron head that weighed 15 pounds.[6] David was armed only with his sling and five smooth stones. The two exchanged threats. David says, 'You come against me with sword and spear and shield; I, however, come against you in the name of the Lord, the army of God, and the host of Israel'.[7] And then David struck him in the forehead with a stone, knocked him down and cut off his head with Goliath's own sword, thus revealing God's favour to David. The Philistines fled.

This duel has a superficial resemblance to the duel of Menelaus and Paris in the *Iliad*, in which the winner would also take all, but, in the *Iliad*, Menelaus is not a giant and he receives no aid from Zeus. In truth, Menelaus needs no such aid, because he is the superior warrior and so will win – and, indeed, he would have killed Paris, if Paris had not been hustled off the battlefield by Aphrodite. In the *Iliad* we have no impossibly massive armament, no gigantic figure, no underdog with a chance of victory. In the *Iliad* the best warriors win unless opposed by a god or outnumbered by the enemy. Battle is a confused melee with champion meeting champion, and the epic is filled with outsized personalities exhibiting courage and cowardice, exhilaration, exhaustion and sweat, death and, sometimes, horrible wounds, but the heroes are all too human.

The *Iliad* was the source and the beginning of western war-and-battle description. True, it is the culmination of a long (now lost) tradition of oral Greek epic, but, nonetheless, it stands alone. It – together with the *Odyssey* – is a unique work of genius. The very nature of the *Iliad* is different from every other account before it, so different that it is hard to exaggerate just how different it is. It seems modern in a way no preceding account does, because all western literature derives from it (and from the *Odyssey*). Although the *Iliad* is an account of an episode in the tenth year of the Trojan War, it tells the whole story of the war in flashbacks and forecasts: the causes, the marshalling of the host – it provides a catalogue of the participants; the negotiations for peace; and the amount of time the two sides have been fighting. Homer describes battle in intimate detail: what the combatants wore, their weapons, their feelings about the battle, individual combat, wounds, noise, death, burial and funeral rites.

The events in the *Iliad* are generated and directed by the intentions and plans of the gods: Aphrodite compels Helen to run off with Paris; Menelaus seeks revenge for the violation of the laws of hospitality, enforced by Zeus; Agamemnon sacrifices his daughter so the gods will give him a fair wind to sail to Troy; and Apollo defends his priest and punishes the Greeks with a plague which leads to an assembly where Agamemnon and Achilles quarrel. Events begin and end with the gods but, nonetheless, the heroes act within this nexus of divine action as though they have free will and can plan and make decisions and carry them out, all the while accepting the power and primacy of the gods.

The heroes are larger-than-life individuals, moved by human emotion, glorying in their prowess, but conscious of the fragility of human existence. Their exaggerated individualism is a Greek characteristic, which the Spartan lawgiver Lycurgus tried to suppress for the better functioning of the Spartan state and the Spartan army. The Spartan poet and general Tyrtaeus drew on the *Iliad* to define the citizen-soldier: 'If one has not seen battle up close, I care nothing for him' and he is the first to write that the young man who dies in the front rank for his state is beautiful.[8] Elsewhere the very un-Spartan soldier–poet Archilochus used the material of his own life – and a sometimes discreditable life it was, too – to compose his songs: throwing away his shield; pursuing his ex-fiancée and her father with invective until they committed suicide; and numerous sexual exploits.[9] His songs were famed throughout the Greek world, sung at every drinking party, praised and criticised, widely imitated and timeless – a joke he related, of which we have only the punch line, was told in slightly altered form in the Infantry School at Ft. Benning.[10]

Three centuries separate Homer from Herodotus. In those centuries the burden of war had shifted from the strictly aristocratic warrior to the middle-class, non-aristocratic citizen fighting alongside his general in a phalanx. Victory was a corporate victory won by group courage and prowess and demanding the subordination of the individual to the unit, although after the battle the survivors voted which individuals had been the bravest. Neither Homer nor Herodotus, nor Greeks in general, were influenced by Near Eastern military accounts and art. Greeks, for instance, knew nothing of Assyrian siege craft and did not systematically study siege craft until the fourth century BC.

As Greeks emphasised their individualism, defended the independence of their little city-states, believed in a religion that was expressed in action and enjoyed the freedom to travel, some sixth century Greek thinkers drew upon Babylonian and Egyptian astronomical records to develop the fundamental questions of modern science. These first philosophers exhibited equal amounts of intellectual arrogance and curiosity, even as their explanations of the creation were little more than standard creation myths with the gods removed.

Greeks also discovered how similar their stories were to the stories of other cultures, with the exception that, whereas a Greek aristocrat traced his ancestry back 15 generations to a god, an Egyptian king could trace his ancestry back 300 generations. These Greek travellers had to conclude that either they, as a people, were very, very young, or that something was amiss with their genealogies. The foremost of these travellers and writers in the fifth century was Herodotus.

Herodotus, three centuries after Homer, composed the first great prose work of western literature, the account of the Persian Wars. The *Histories*, like the *Iliad*, is unique in its time for its beauty, its content and its creativity. Herodotus, the 'father of history', is the first to inquire into both the events and the causes of events. As earlier authors proclaimed their individuality and the centrality of their own emotional experiences, and the natural philosophers rejected mythical explanations and proclaimed the primacy of human intelligence in understanding the earth and the cosmos, so Herodotus looked to human explanations for human events.

Herodotus adopted Homer's viewpoint as a detached observer and reporter of the conflict, reporting equally – and mostly impartially – from both sides. Herodotus – with Homer – established the convention for describing battles: a list of the combatants' national origins; the organisation of the battle line; the course of the battle; and the result. (As for the experience of combat, he omitted what every one of his readers would have experienced for himself.) Herodotus relates much more than battles and wars, but always the wars are the unifying and central theme of his work. To Homer, Herodotus, Thucydides (the successor of Herodotus) and subsequent historians, war and the politics of war were the primary and most important subjects.

In the world as Herodotus saw it, the gods do not appear to men, but a divine fate is woven into human existence and lies behind every major event – although, within that circumscribed fate, human beings have room to act independently and to make decisions and plans, or to choose between alternate fates, as Achilles did. Herodotus believed that the oracles of Delphi were true, as were omens and signs, but they were open to interpretation by individuals.

As Herodotus enters a period of history in which he could have interviewed eyewitnesses, human decisions seem to become more important. In the campaign at Marathon, for instance, the Persians chose to land at Marathon, after which they received some omens – obvious only after the event – which predicted that they would fail. The Athenians seized a blocking position and they won the battle because – Herodotus makes this clear – of the decisions they made. They debated their plan of action – the ten generals were divided five-five – and Miltiades convinced the polemarch (the 'commander-in-chief') to authorise an attack.

As Herodotus describes the battle, the greatest risk for the Athenians was their exposure to the Persian archers as they advanced, so – for the first time in a Greek battle – they charged at a run ('almost a mile'). While running, the two flanks bunched up and the centre became weak enough that the Persians could break through. Herodotus states broadly that the fighting was hard and he gives a few details – an Athenian named Cynegirus had his hand cut off with an axe as he attempted to keep a Persian ship on shore. (Cynegirus was the brother of Aeschylus.) An Athenian reported that in the midst of the fighting, without receiving a blow or a wound, he suddenly encountered a superhuman figure and went blind. Herodotus reports the number of casualties. The Athenians lost 192 men and they killed 6,400 Persians (a number verified, Herodotus writes, because the polemarch had vowed to sacrifice a kid for every Persian killed). Herodotus concludes that one man was responsible for the victory and that man was Miltiades.

Herodotus does not conceal his admiration for some individuals. He learned the names of each of the 300 Spartans at Thermopylae, and he reserved particular praise for the Spartan king Leonidas who decided to remain at Thermopylae and fight to the death in order, Herodotus suggests, to fulfil a Delphic prophesy that had set out two alternate fates for Sparta: a king would die or the city would fall. On the other hand, his treatment of Xerxes, the arch-enemy of the Greeks, is not unsympathetic – supernatural forces (the personification of Fate perhaps) compelled Xerxes to invade Greece against his better judgement.

For the battle of Plataea as for Marathon, he relates the forces involved on each side, who the leaders were, what they thought and felt and said, what decisions they made, to what extent they were influenced by their soothsayers and how their decisions led step by step to the final confrontation. He relates the personal histories of the two Elean soothsayers; how one hated the Spartans and the other became a Spartan citizen and how both advised against an attack – Mardonius, the Persian commander, accepted his soothsayer's pronouncement with impatience, because he was convinced that the Spartans were more reputation than substance and he was eager to fight them.

The Greek commander, the Spartan regent Pausanias, decided to withdraw to a better position, but a junior commander Amompharetus refused and they bickered through most of the night. 'The stubborn Amompharetus with both hands picked up a boulder from the ground, dropped it at Pausanias' feet, and declared, that with this "ballot" he voted not to move'.[11] Pausanias told him he had lost his senses and started without him, at which point Amompharetus followed slowly. When Mardonius learned that the Spartans had withdrawn, he called them cowards and ordered everyone to pursue as fast as they could.

The Spartans were caught in the open as the Persian forces massed against them. The Spartan soothsayer pronounced that the signs for the battle were adverse and Pausanias ordered the Spartans to protect themselves with their shields, but not to take any offensive action. While the Spartans were defending themselves, one Spartan, Callicrates, 'the handsomest man in the army', was struck by an arrow in his side and taken to the rear where he spoke his last words; he did not regret that he was dying for Greece, but that 'he did not accomplish any great deed as he had wished so much to do'.[12] The soothsayer took another reading, declared that the signs were now favourable, and the Spartans charged. A vicious fight followed and the Persians held out for as long as Mardonius continued to fight, but when he was killed they broke and ran. Herodotus lists the most prominent individuals killed on both sides, which Spartans were especially distinguished for their bravery and how the brave were honoured in ceremonies after the battle.

Herodotus' successor, Thucydides, seems to come from another world. In his world the earliest natural philosophers had already removed the gods from nature, the first historian had removed the gods from politics and war and physicians had placed disease in the natural world with natural causes. Thucydides' contemporary, Socrates, posed the question, if human events are caused by human decisions and actions, what about human custom and law? Do our laws come down from heaven? Or are laws strictly a human invention? If the laws are only human, then there is no moral wrong (in the divine sense) in violating them nor will there be a divine retribution, only the practical consequence, if caught, of being punished by men. Thus Socrates' dilemma was, *in the absence of gods, what is justice?*

Thucydides expected his audience to be familiar with both Homer and Herodotus, he was literate in contemporary medicine, raised in a sceptical Athens and shaken by the experience of the plague which struck down the pious and impious equally. He set out to write a history of the Peloponnesian War with the same care that a physician would exercise in taking a history of a patient. He sought the best evidence, he interviewed eyewitnesses, he strove to give exact figures for the men involved on each side of a battle for each national contingent and he described as exactly as he could what happened. He concluded that his history was worth writing because of the dimensions of the war and also because his history would be a kind of case study, which would be valuable in the future when similar events were sure to occur. He asserted – and he was right – that his would be a work which would last forever.[13]

The gods and Fate were allowed no part in Thucydides' account and he mentions omens and prodigies only when they are material to the story, as when at Syracuse, with the survival of the Athenian fleet in question, Nicias, the Athenian commander, was influenced by a lunar eclipse (on 27 August 413 BC). 'Nicias – he was entirely too susceptible to divination and such things – said that he would not even discuss matters before, as the soothsayers advised, thrice nine days had passed'.[14] His intransigence led directly to the destruction of the Athenian fleet.

Thucydides describes what the leaders of each side and, sometimes, the men in the ranks, were thinking. He writes, for instance, that the Spartans could not remember ever being as surprised as they were, when they saw an enemy formation suddenly appear on the plain of Mantinea.[15]

Nonetheless, the Spartans got organised and won the battle. As for the number of Spartans at that battle, Thucydides gives his calculations, but adds – 'The size of their army is considered a state secret'.[16]

Tactics interested Thucydides. He described how Pagondas the Theban at the battle of Delium (424 BC) was the first to employ cavalry to outflank (and surprise) a phalanx, the first to direct a deep attack at a particular point and, later, the first to use a flamethrower (to burn down an Athenian fortification). Pagondas' combination of cavalry and infantry influenced Epaminondas (the Theban general who devised the tactical scheme which defeated the Spartans at the battle of Leuctra), and Epaminondas, in turn, influenced Philip and Alexander, the masters of tactics.

Victor Davis Hanson, an historian of ancient military matters, attributes the beginning of tactics to Pagondas.[17] This attribution is open to argument, certainly, but it could not be made at all without the account of Thucydides. Memory is fragile and survives in detail only through written records. The fighting of the Trojan War – if, indeed, there was such a war – is remembered not because the war was so important, but because of the *Iliad*. Other greater wars are known only by deduction: the chariot people's conquest of Greece, the Mycenaean conquest of Crete (reflected perhaps in the legend of Theseus and the Minotaur) and the destruction of the Mycenaean civilisation itself.

Herodotus and Thucydides were the first in a long line of historians from their own day to ours. Herodotus' work remains a pleasure to read (and a valuable source for the Persian wars, too) and Thucydides' meticulous and fluent account remains a model for modern historians. If he appears to be less influential today, it is because the methods he created are now accepted practice. Since his time we have had many fine historians, innovators of style and inventors of new fields but, in the end, as the Israeli military historian Martin van Creveld says, 'When it comes to the writing of military history, Classical antiquity has never been surpassed'.[18] These first two historians bequeathed to all of humanity an immeasurable legacy.

Thucydides' successor was the Athenian Xenophon, who has left us, among other works, a sort of personal history of his own time and a memoir (see below) of his participation in the expedition of Cyrus the Younger. He knew the leaders personally, he was experienced in war and he participated in some of the battles and events he describes. He had his heroes – first Socrates, then Cyrus and, finally, the Spartan king, Agesilaus, and he does not conceal his biases. He despised the Thebans (his hero Agesilaus hated them) and thought the Theban defeat of the Spartans was the worst possible thing that could have happened. However, he could not help but admire the ability of the Theban general Epaminondas and he praised him for seeking battle and glory.

Xenophon describes the intimate details only a veteran would know – before the battle of Mantinea in 362 BC he describes the cavalry whitening their helmets and the Arcadian hoplites polishing their shields, inscribing clubs on them (like Thebans) and sharpening the blades of their spears and swords. Epaminondas feigned an encampment, then suddenly formed up and advanced, catching his enemy by surprise. Xenophon described their panicked state of mind – 'none of them were calm, they ran about, putting bits in their horses mouths, and bridling them, putting on their breastplates, and acting more like men who expect something bad to happen to them than to do bad to others'.[19] He describes how hard it is to rally men who see others on their side running. And, of course, he describes the battle. The Thebans were pushing the Spartans back and the Spartans appeared to be breaking, then Epaminondas received a mortal wound, and the Thebans stopped. Both sides claimed victory.

Herodotus, Thucydides and Xenophon established the standard for reporting wars and battles: name the forces and the leaders; detail their dispositions and their plans; describe the battle in general terms; give some intimate details; explain who won and why; list the number of casualties (dead, not wounded); and describe the immediate aftermath of the battle. They may also have created the impression that wars are fought in a series of battles – or even one crucial battle – rather than by following an overarching strategy of which battles are a component.

In their own day these historians inspired many imitators, although the works of most of the historians of the fourth and third centuries are lost

– some are remembered only by their names and some survive only in scattered fragments. They suffered from several defects (in the opinion of later generations) – they did not write the Attic Greek of Thucydides and Xenophon and they wrote about a period of decline which Greeks preferred to forget. The historian Theopompus, for instance, suspended his history of Greece to travel north to Macedonia to write about Philip; he was criticised for abandoning the sublime subject of Greece to write about one disreputable foreigner. (His work, the *Philippica*, is lost.) Nonetheless, these early writers established 'historian' as a profession and 'history' as a field of study.

By the second century the Greek historian Polybius could offer a (self-serving) definition – the writer of politics and war should seek the testimonies of eyewitnesses, memoirs and documents and, where possible, conduct a personal inspection of the topography of the battlefield, but, before all else, he should be a man with some political and some military experience. A would-be historian without practical experience, Polybius writes, can no more compose history based solely on records of the past than a would-be artist can create works of art just by examining past works of art.[20] Without experience, Polybius' rival historians, as he delights in pointing out, fall constantly into error, and thus fall short of the most important quality of history – truth.[21] History, when well done, will provide the reader not only with knowledge of the past and moral examples to guide his own life, but also with a practical guide to action in the future.[22]

The last Greek (language) classical historian whose work is significant, well-written and extant is Arrian, a Greek who served as a Roman officer under Hadrian; he called himself the new Xenophon, studied philosophy under Epictetus and wrote an account of Alexander the Great (whom he admired) from two contemporary accounts: Aristoboulos and Ptolemy. His account is both detailed and personal. For instance, at Gaugamela, he writes that the campfires of the army of Darius filled the whole horizon and,

Some say that Parmenion came into the king's tent and advised a night attack on the Persians. He said that a night attack is a fearsome thing and it would surprise and terrify them. Alexander replied to him – and there were others in the tent who heard this – that it would be shameful to steal victory and it was necessary that Alexander win openly and without any trick.[23]

In the morning Alexander led his army out to battle.

Arrian gives his own opinion from his own experience that a night attack can easily go wrong and the aggressor can lose just because of the difficulties of coordination. Arrian also explains how he knows what he knows: he can describe the Persian order of battle because the order came into Macedonian possession after the battle.

Roman historians followed Greek tradition. (The first of them wrote in Greek.) The first Roman historian whose works survive in any measure – two essays on the Jugurthine War and the Conspiracy of Catiline – is Sallust (86–35 BC). The first Roman historian whose work survives to a considerable extent is Livy (59 BC–AD 17). Livy was exactly the sort of historian Polybius professed to despise; a man without experience who researched his history in the library (so to speak). He wrote a history of Rome – a prose epic from the founding of Rome to his own time – in 142 books, of which 35 survive. It is a notable literary work – he was a master storyteller – and was widely influential. His Latin is relatively easy to translate for sense, but extremely difficult for style. For example, he reports that the announcement of the defeat of the Romans at Trasimene was delivered by a praetor in the following words, *'pugna magna victi sumus.'*[24] A translation is easy – 'We have been defeated in a great battle' – but the easy translation misses the suspense of the announcement in Latin: *pugna* – there was a battle; *magna* – it was a big one; *victi* – someone was defeated; *sumus* – it was us!

In his description of the battle of Cannae, Livy describes the rivalry between the two Roman leaders, Varro and Paullus.[25] Hannibal was trying to lure the Romans into a battle on ground suitable for cavalry. Varro accused his colleague of timidity, or worse. His troops, he said, were eager to fight, only Paullus stood in the way of a great victory. Paullus pointed out the examples of the rash commanders at the two Roman catastrophes, the Trebia and Trasimene. When it was Varro's turn to command he set out with his troops and Paullus followed out of a sense of duty. Livy describes the movements of Hannibal, the organisation of his army, the fact that the wind was blowing dust into the faces of the Romans, the clash of the armies, the encirclement of the Romans, the slaughter, the flight of Varro, and the heroic speech and death of Paullus. On the next day the Carthaginians inspected the battlefield.

> There they lay, so many thousands of Romans, infantry and cavalry indiscriminately mixed, wherever the fortunes of war or flight had taken them. Some covered in blood rose from the heaps of dead, aroused by the cool of dawn – they were struck down by the enemy. Some lying there alive with the tendons in their legs cut, bared their throats and asked them to release the little blood they had left; some had buried their heads in the dirt, in order to suffocate themselves. The one incident that especially struck the Carthaginians was the still-living Numidian, with his face horribly bitten, lying under a dead Roman, whose hands no longer could hold a weapon, but whose ferocious anger had caused him to lacerate the enemy with his teeth.[26]

The next great – some scholars say the greatest – Roman historian, Tacitus (AD 56–117), wrote two major works, the *Histories*, of which four and a quarter books survive (covering the years AD 69–70), and the *Annals*, of which Books 1–4, 6, and the last half of 11 to the first half of 16 (from the death of Augustus to Nero) survive. Tacitus is more interested in the politics of Rome than in its wars, and he is particularly interested in the characters and personalities of the leaders and their followers and opponents. He denounces the credulity of human nature in believing prophecies and the harm that that credulity did, for instance, in the mind of Otho, who believed in an imperial destiny predicted for himself.[27] Tacitus is a master of the brief phrase loaded with meaning and almost impossible to translate.

'Galba,' he writes, as Otho was being proclaimed emperor in the praetorian camp, 'implored the gods of the Roman Empire which already
belonged to another (*fatigabat alieni iam imperii deos*)'.[28] His description
of the machinations of Otho against Galba are masterful, the swaying of
the crowd ready to applaud this man or that man, whoever appeared to be
winning, the spread of the rumour (that Otho had been killed) by men
who heard the rumour and then claimed to be eyewitnesses – one soldier
even came before Galba with a bloody sword and claimed to have done
the deed – the conflicting advice, the exhilaration and despair and the uncer-
tainty of the soldiers, who held the real power.

Otho stretched out his hands to the mob of soldiers, bowed to them,
blew them kisses and 'played the slave in order to become their master'.[29]
Meanwhile the supporters of Galba were making 'plans for circumstances
which had already passed'.[30] Tacitus summarises the character of Galba in
a famous phrase noted for its brevity and complexity – he says that everyone
believed that Galba would have been just the man to be emperor if he had
not, in fact, been emperor (*omnium consensu capex imperii, nisi imperasset*).[31]
While Tacitus is less interested in battle and more interested in politics,
nonetheless he wrote a brilliant (literary) description of the battle at
Cremona.[32] Tacitus was much admired by Machiavelli.

The last of the great classical historians is Ammianus Marcellinus. He
was a pagan in an increasingly Christianised world and he was disturbed
by the corruption and incompetence he saw at all levels of society. In 378,
after the Romans had admitted the Goths into the Roman Empire, with
the understanding that the Goths would defend the line of the Danube
against the Huns, the Romans mistreated the Goths and the Goths attacked
the Romans. The Roman emperor Valens brought his army from
Adrianopolis. He declined to wait for his nephew, the emperor of the West,
and reached the laager of the Goths while a large part of their cavalry was
absent. Valens frittered away his opportunity to catch the Goths at a disad-
vantage while at the same time exposing his own troops to hunger and
thirst. When the two sides engaged, the Roman cavalry was defeated and
the Roman infantry was left to fend for itself.

Our soldiers, with the utmost contempt of death, struck down the enemy with their swords and were struck down themselves, and, on both sides, men's helmets and breastplates were split with the blows of axes.[33]

At last the infantry broke too and the army turned in panicked flight.

The roads were blocked by the wounded, half-dead and crying out with their suffering. And, in addition to them, were the heaps of slain horses. The bodies of men and horses filled the plain.[34]

Valens was killed, but his body was not found. The battle of Adrianople was a catastrophe from which the Roman Empire never fully recovered.

These historians followed a literary tradition begun with Homer, a tradition which was passed down from them through successions of civilisations in the west to the present day. Polybius' definition of the historian prevailed into the twentieth century, and although *historian* became a separate profession, many historians lacked military experience, and some even eschewed such experience, while they agreed with him that the business of the historian is politics and war ... and the truth.

Today the military historian generally assumes a viewpoint from above (like Homer), sets the scene, gives an overview of the war, campaign, or battle and then adds the views or experiences of the soldiers actually engaged in the battle.

To be sure, other ancient literary authors wrote about war: poets like Silius Italicus (a sterile account of the Second Punic War, the *Punica*); biographers like Plutarch; rhetoricians; orators; philosophers; generals; and adventurers. Some ancient historians injected personal views or even personal experiences into their writing. Ammianus Marcellinus relates a personal anecdote which reveals the abysmal stupidity of the Roman upper class and Polybius is quick to assess and criticise other historians and political leaders. Other authors related their own personal war experiences in detail and at length – Xenophon's *Anabasis*, Caesar's *Gallic* and *Civil Wars*, and Josephus' *Jewish War*. Xenophon's *Anabasis* is the first (extant) war memoir. Caesar's are the only extant accounts of a commanding general. These three created the idea and the pattern for the modern military memoir.

A modern guide defines a memoir as 'a story from a life. It makes no pretense of replicating a whole life'. The reader of a memoir [the author writes] looks for an 'adept storyteller', a theme, 'a shapely whole', and 'a voice that captures a personality'. In short, readers should feel that they are being 'spoken to'. A memoirist

> has a contract with the reader. You say, 'This really happened.' [. . .]
> The memoir must be limited to one time and one experience (your own, of course)'.[35]

The *Anabasis* could form an exemplar for this definition of a memoir.

Xenophon writes about his own experiences through the whole of the *Anabasis*, but, because the account would be read aloud, either by the reader to himself or to an audience, he refers to himself in the third person. He introduces himself when he begins to play an active part in the expedition of Cyrus, son of Darius, against his older brother, King Artaxerxes. In the first book Xenophon explains the circumstances and the evolution of the campaign. Xenophon was there as an observer, but he became a participant after the battle, when the Greek generals were murdered and he was elected as one of the new generals. He describes the retreat from beginning to end, the major encounters, the difficulties and also the interesting places he visited. After an exhausting march through the snow, the Greeks came to a village.

> The homes were underground, the entrance was like a well, but widening out below. A separate entrance for the animals had been dug, men went down a ladder. In their houses were goats, sheep, cattle, fowl, and the offspring of these. They all fed from food stored underground. There was wheat, barley, beans and 'barley-wine' [beer] in big bowls. The bowls were brimming and there were straws.

Whenever one was thirsty he just drank from a straw. It was very strong, but once you got used to it, it wasn't bad.[36]

Unlike the *Anabasis,* Caesar's account of the Gallic Wars is not exactly a memoir, but a series of reports (*Commentaries*) to the Senate about an ongoing campaign. Other Roman commanders wrote accounts of their campaigns and submitted them to the Senate, but his is the only one to survive. (Livy may have used Cato's *Commentaries* in describing the war in Spain and Josephus may have used those of Vespasian and Titus in composing his *Jewish Wars*.) Caesar's *Commentaries* survive, perhaps, as much because of his fame and his beautiful Latin prose style, as because of the material. They were reintroduced in Europe in the Renaissance, translated into French in 1488, German in 1507 and English in 1530, and have not been out of print since.[37]

In one example of his writing in Book II, Caesar describes a surprise attack made by the Nervii on his army just as it was preparing camp. Caesar took personal charge of two legions, the twelfth and the seventh, which were particularly hard pressed. In one cohort all the centurions had been killed and in the others most were wounded or killed.

Caesar took a shield from one of the newest recruits, because he had come without his shield, and he moved into the front ranks [of the twelfth], and he called upon each centurion by name, and he ordered the rest of the soldiers to rally by the standards, and he ordered them to open their formation, so they could use their swords more easily. His presence brought hope to the soldiers and reinvigorated their spirit, since each soldier in this extreme danger wanted to distinguish himself in the presence of his commander. Caesar, when he saw that the seventh legion was hard pressed by the enemy, advised the military tribunes that, little by little, they should bring the two legions together, back to back, and turn the standards on the enemy. When that was done, the soldiers lost their fear that they would be surrounded and they began to stand their ground and fight bravely.[38]

Caesar's *Commentaries* legitimised the personal account.

Josephus (born *c.* AD 37) was a Jewish general who opposed the Romans in the reign of Nero. When the future emperor Vespasian (r. AD 69–79) arrived in Judaea to take command of the Roman operations there, Josephus quickly realised that the Jewish forces were totally outmatched and so, after futile attempts to convince the Jewish authorities in Jerusalem that they hadn't a chance, he looked for a way to surrender himself to the Romans while still keeping his dignity intact.[39] He writes that he came over to the Romans not as a deserter, but as a 'minister of God' who foretold these events in his dreams. He was the first to hail Vespasian as emperor and, when Vespasian did become emperor, he was freed and granted Roman citizenship.[40] Josephus remained in the entourage of Vespasian, so he was a witness to the events of the war and he wrote a self-serving account of the Jewish Wars, beginning in the third book with his own involvement. He recounts the horrific siege of Jerusalem and of Masada. He also wrote an account of the *Antiquities of the Jews* and a brief autobiography. He was not an historian of the first, or perhaps even the second rank, but his subject matter was of great interest to Christian Europe and, because of that, his work became influential.

Surviving personal accounts are rare, eyewitness accounts even rarer and accounts by anyone not in the well-to-do, well-educated class almost non-existent. *The Spanish War* by 'Caesar' appears to have been written by a soldier, perhaps a centurion (whose work would never have survived had it not been attributed to Julius Caesar). Aeschylus includes several observations which only a veteran would know – about lice, for instance! – and a kind of eyewitness account of the battle of Salamis. In the *Persians* a 'messenger' tells the Persian royal family what happened at Salamis. This passage is one of our few direct eyewitness accounts of ancient warfare, although it is transferred from the memory of Aeschylus to the mouth of a Persian and transformed into tragic verse. In the *Acharnians* Aristophanes satirises the veterans of Marathon, who form his chorus and are forever boasting about the battle (and thereby boring everyone else).

The survival of literature depended both on the literacy and the class of those who made the decisions to copy and preserve manuscripts and, as both literary Latin and Greek became frozen in style and diction, authors outside the canon had little chance that their works would survive. However, Greeks and Romans did write memoirs (for instance, Agrippina,[41] and the Achaean statesman Aratus,[42] both now lost). Of all the ancient authors, not surprisingly, Caesar was the most influential. The publisher of the memoirist Roger Williams (*Actions of the Lowe Countries*, 1618) notes that one reason for publishing his memoirs was 'to incite other men of Armes to imitate in like sort their great master, Julius Caesar.'[43] Although the inspiration for the memoir came from Caesar (and to a lesser degree Xenophon and Josephus), the form of the memoir reflected the culture and experience of individuals in different periods. Military memoirists of the Medieval and Renaissance periods described great actions and great deeds, but were uninterested in any careful explanation of cause and effect, strategy and tactics, or logistics.[44]

In the Medieval period, such luminaries as Jean de Joinville (1225–1317, the Egyptian Crusade) and Geoffrey de Villehardouin (1150–1213, the Fourth Crusade) wrote their personal reminiscences within their more general accounts of the Crusades; Walter the Chancellor (*Bella Antiochena*) and Gerald of Wales (*Expugnatio Hibernica*) modelled their works on the *wars* of Julius Caesar.[45] Less formal memoirs also survive– knights recounted tales of their adventures and, in some cases, members of their audience wrote them down.

In Renaissance France the writing of memoirs, and the name itself, became so popular that some scholars have argued that the genre was a creation of that period and place, but the prominent memoirists themselves refer back to exemplars in the ancient world. Both Guillaume du Bellay (to Thucydides and Xenophon) and Rene de Bellay (to Thucydides and Caesar) trace a line of memoirists from these first writers to themselves.[46] One of the most striking of the memoirs was Bernal Diaz del Castillo's account of the conquest of Mexico (1514–21): 'That which I, myself, have seen and the fighting I have gone through, with the help of God, I will describe quite simply, as a fair eyewitness without twisting events one way or another.'[47]

Later generations, who studied the classics as the fundamental basis of their education, consciously imitated ancient authors. A comparison of ancient, Renaissance and modern memoirs exposes the different views of battle and war – modern military memoirs, by and large, are concerned with individual experience, Renaissance memoirs more with events.[48]

Soldiers, then and now, have not changed much. They know only what happens to them as individuals and they are not necessarily reliable witnesses. Thucydides was involved in some of the events and he interviewed eyewitnesses and checked their accounts with others ... and discovered that eyewitnesses to the same event often gave different accounts, both because of imperfect memory and because of personal bias.[49] In the Greek world a man writing about his experiences in war was addressing an audience who would have had similar experiences. According to Pericles, that audience had little patience for the stories of others, but what else would a veteran have to write about? Individual soldiers seldom have a grasp of the whole picture. As Guillaume Cretin has the Marshall of Chabannes say,

But do you think that soldiers in battle
In the hour when they stand in the very midst of combat
When men strive with great blows to completely cleave them asunder
Think of anything except to defend themselves?[50]

Soldiers in the ancient world arrayed in a tight-packed formation smelled blood and excrement, heard the cries of men 'killing and being killed' and the clash of arms, and they saw the enemy, but still, no less, their experience was confined to themselves, those to each side, and those directly in front of them. Archilochus composed songs about his life as a soldier – he leaned upon his spear to drink, he earned his living with his spear; he wanted a commander with sturdy legs and guts, not a pretty-boy who curled his hair; he threw away his shield – but we hardly know what battles or what wars he fought in and he doesn't describe strategy or tactics.

Soldiers today – by 'today' I mean the soldiers of the twentieth and twenty-first centuries – no less than soldiers in the ancient world, have a limited perspective. They see those to their left and right, they fire their weapons into the space in front of them, where they think the enemy is located, they hear the crack of bullets, they smell the munitions. Today's soldiers, if they serve in a well-led unit, will know their immediate objective and what they each must do. They probably will not know any greater objective than 'we are going here and doing this'. Herman Wouk expresses this reality in *The Caine Mutiny* when he writes that his hero, Willie Keith,

> was on his way to fight in battles as great as any in the histories. But these would appear to him mere welters of nasty, complicated, tiresome activity. Only in after years, reading books describing the scenes in which he had been engaged, would he begin to think of his battles as Battles.[51]

The generals will have a broader knowledge, of course, but they seldom share the strategic plan with their men; rather they say whatever might move their men to fight. Alexander briefed his officers on his plan of battle at Issus and what they were to do, and he encouraged them, each according to his own interests, including the possibility of loot and the weakness of the enemy – they were fighting Persians and in the end the 'Persians have Darius and you have Alexander'.[52] When, however, the battle line was drawn up, Alexander rode from one end to the other and encouraged his army by calling on the officers by name and also the men and units who had shown their bravery . . . and they responded, 'Attack!'[53]

The 'modern' military memoir, that is, the memoir written by authors who, in describing their own experiences, also describe their state of mind, began in the eighteenth century and flourished during the Napoleonic Wars.[54] European officers, and British officers, in particular, who served in World War I, had received a classical education and, in their letters to newspapers, casual references in private letters and their literary efforts, they readily quoted, and even composed, Latin and Greek verse.[55] They – and the German youths in *All Quiet on the Western Front* – go to war urged on by their school masters.[56] The classics permeated all classes of society.[57]

One of the advantages of reading a number of memoirs from the ancient world to the present is the similarities behind the motives of the authors for going to war: Xenophon, Joseph Plumb Martin (the American Revolution) and Audie Murphey (World War II) went for the adventure . . . as did I. Most memoirs conclude with the end of the war, the campaign, or, in Xenophon's case, the dissolution of the army of mercenaries. The essence of war memoir is the story of the author's experiences in war and is not, therefore, an account of a war or even of a battle.

Modern accounts of wars, campaigns and battles combine the view from above with memoirs and photographs to try to give a complete and rounded account. Cornelius Ryan's *The Longest Day* set the standard for modern historical accounts. His narrative shifts back and forth between the allied and the German point of view with many personal anecdotes. His title, for instance, comes from a quotation of Erwin Rommel.[58] His approach reflects both Homer and Herodotus.

In addition to histories and memoirs there are also many novels, far too many to cover in one part of one chapter. Here I mention some of the latest works and also some of my favourites. The selection is personal and idiosyncratic: I have read widely, if not comprehensively. Three novelists – Stephen Pressfield (*The Afghan Campaign*), Mary Renault (*The Persian Boy*) and L. Sprague de Camp (*An Elephant for Aristotle*) – of different periods and genres have written about Alexander from different perspectives. L. Sprague de Camp is a science-fiction writer who developed an interest in the ancient world and wrote some non-fiction books on the subject, for example *The Ancient Engineers*. In *An Elephant for Aristotle*, Alexander assigns a Thessalian officer the job of taking an elephant back to Athens so Aristotle can examine it.

Several authors have also written about the Persian Wars and the Spartans. Stephen Pressfield has written *Gates of Fire* about Thermopylae. Gene Wolfe is a popular science-fiction writer whose *Soldier of Arete* is, oddly enough, about a Roman soldier who suffered a head wound at the battle of Plataea and can remember only what happens in one waking period. His wound gives him the ability to see the ghosts and gods of Greece. Helena P. Schrader has written a series about the Spartan king Leonidas, the first of which is *Leonidas of Sparta: A Boy of the Agoge*. A number of novels have taken their inspiration from the Trojan War including one by Dan Simmons, *Ilium*, set on Mars.

Many authors have chosen to place their stories in the Roman world. In *Ranks of Bronze*, David Drake, a Vietnam veteran, imagines an alien civilisation which buys the Roman survivors of the campaign of Crassus and uses them to fight wars under particular conventions which limit the weapons allowed. He has also written a series whose hero is Belisarius. Harry Turtledove, trained in Byzantine history, achieved success with a series in which a Roman legion – and one Gaul – are transported to another world modelled on the Byzantine Empire, except with magic. *The Misplaced Legion* is the first in the 'Videssos Cycle' series.

Harry Sidebottom has a series, *Warrior of Rome*, set in the mid-east in the third century AD. The hero is a northern barbarian who has been granted Roman citizenship and the command of an outpost on the Euphrates River in AD 256. He has to defend the town from a Sassanid attack. The author is a lecturer at Oxford in the field of ancient warfare and has a good command of the period and of siege warfare. A number of novels and series of novels are set in the time of Julius Caesar. One of the most interesting is Alfred Duggan's *Winter Quarters* about a troop of Gallic cavalry who fight for Caesar and wind up in the army of Crassus in the east, and one of the most popular is Colleen McCullough's series about Julius Caesar, *First Man in Rome*.

These, then, are just a smattering of the novels available. A person of generous reading habits could spend a year reading only those novels set in the ancient world and still have plenty left for the next year and the next, but I would be remiss not to recommend to readers Homer, Herodotus and Thucydides. I read Thucydides when I was 12 and I loved it. I thought it was a heroic fantasy but true.

CHAPTER VI

IMAGES OF WAR

The first extant depiction of a historical military event appears on the palette of Narmer.[1] The palette of Narmer is about two feet high and in the form of a conventional cosmetic palette, but is too large to serve that function. The king, twice the size of any other figure, does the fighting, stacks up headless corpses and, with the help of the (other) gods, captures cities. Because 'Narmer' wears the crown of Upper Egypt on one side and the crown of Lower Egypt on the other, the scenes have been interpreted – not without some controversy – as a representation of the unification of Egypt by the early king, Narmer. The palette is typical of the sorts of evidence found in the ancient Near East, including: the early Stele of the Vultures (2500–2400 BC) showing a phalanx led by a god (probably) advancing across a field of corpses; the Standard of Ur (c.2500 BC) showing individual soldiers, carts, corpses, booty and feasting; and the Stele of Rimush (c.2270 BC) depicting soldiers armed with bow, sword and spear, with one soldier cutting the throat of another with his sword. All come from Sumer and Akkad.[2] The later Assyrian reliefs (c. 900–600 BC) are an extensive and detailed representation of Assyrian military operations. These representations have certain characteristics in common: they stand alone without accompanying literary narrative and they glorify the ruler and the gods.

Art in Greece was quite different, although we do not have the voices of the artists nor, often, any more clues to the purpose of the works depicting war than the work itself, but they complement the literary descriptions that we do have. Thus, in addition to the songs Archilochus composed about his life as a soldier, we can visualise exactly what equipment he had and exactly how he would have appeared fully armed and armoured. War was a constant theme in Greek art.

The art of the age of Homer seems to represent warfare of that period quite realistically. An Attic figural krater (760–750 BC) – a mixing bowl for wine – depicting a 'Homeric' melee shows stacks of naked (that is, stripped) corpses, one warrior about to cut the throat of another with his sword and a warrior with an arrow through his head.[3] The message is, like the *Iliad*, what you make of it – it is brutal, but it is also the common experience of the man who would own such a krater and display it in the centre of his festive table.

The Chigi Vase[4] (seventh century BC) depicts the sequence of events leading up to a hoplite battle – a soldier putting on greaves and another adjusting his helmet, a group running to get into formation behind a flute-player (only the Spartans marched into battle to the sound of flutes) and two lines fighting. By the time of the Chigi Vase, artists had mastered the difficulties of representing a phalanx battle. Earlier artists showed individuals fighting and the viewer had to understand that the individuals represented a line. The vase painters depicted all phases of the battle. The so-called 'C-Painter', for instance, depicts combat with some combatants fleeing, some fallen and one begging for his life.[5]

The 'Kleophon painter' depicts a warrior's departure from home – the libation cup he holds has been filled by his wife.[6] In another vase painting (c.480) the Kleophon painter has depicted the sack of Troy and the killing of a bloodstained Priam who is holding in his lap the bloodstained body of his grandson, Astyanax (the son of Hector).[7] A dead soldier, bloodstained, lies on the floor and in the second scene another Trojan warrior lies dead with his head thrown back. The lesser Aias is about to rape Cassandra who is clutching the altar of Athena while women around lament and Aeneas flees. Here, in brief, is every outrage committed in a captured city.

Douris depicts Eos tending to the corpse of her son, Memnon, before

Zeus grants him immortality.[8] The dead figures, and even the living victims, are decorously presented, although the viewer feels the pathos of the situation. On another vase, two warriors carry home the corpse of a comrade on their shoulders; his head and feet hang down, his eye is open and staring and the artist has artfully suggested the dead weight of the body, acknowledging the impression that the dead are heavier to carry than the living.[9]

These vase paintings are individual possessions, but cities commissioned works of art to publicly acknowledge and celebrate the deeds of the past.[10] The visitor to the Painted Stoa in Athens would first see a gate with a trophy of a victory over the Macedonians and then a painting of a battle scene between the Athenians and the Spartans – the two lines are about to close in hand-to-hand fighting. In the middle was a scene of Theseus and the Athenians fighting the Amazons and then a scene of the victorious Greek leaders at Troy meeting to determine the fate of the lesser Aias, who had raped Cassandra at the altar of Athena. Finally, at the end of the painting was a scene of Marathon. Pausanias, the ultimate tourist, writes,

> The Plataeans and Athenians are closing with the barbarians and the fight is about even here, but in the middle of the battle the barbarians are fleeing and are pushing each other into the swamp while at the end of the painting are the Phoenician ships and the barbarians who are scrambling onboard while the Greeks slaughter them. And here also is drawn the hero Marathon, from whom the district is named, and Theseus arising from the ground, and Athena and Heracles. Of the mortal combatants prominent in the painting are Callimachus, who had been chosen commander-in-chief and Miltiades, one of the generals, and the hero Echetlos.

Also in the painted Stoa were the shields taken from the Spartans at Sphacteria.

The Alexander Mosaic, found in Pompeii, is based on a painting depicting Alexander at the critical moment of a battle against Darius. (Who the expected audience was, is unclear.) Alexander, without helmet so that he can be readily identified and his emotions shown, presses forward towards Darius. He has transfixed a Persian noble with his long spear (the *sarissa*). The noble and his horse have fallen. Darius stretches out his hand towards the dying noble – or perhaps towards Alexander – as his charioteer whips up the horses to carry Darius out of the battle.[11] The artist with one scene has captured the essence of the characters of Alexander and Darius, the aggressiveness of Alexander, the fear and sorrow of Darius, the key moment of the battle and a basic truth: if Darius had not fled, Alexander would have killed him.

In sculpture, the Siphnian Treasury (end of sixth century BC) shows the battle of the Greeks and the Trojans and the battle of the gods and the giants.[12] The thighs of the warriors are massive, and two corpses lie twisted on the ground. The Alexander Sarcophagus (end of fourth century BC) shows the emotions of the combatants in various individual combats, the dead in contorted, but not grotesque, postures while, in contrast, the Pergamum Frieze (first half of second century BC) portrays the agony of those killing and being killed through the contortion of their bodies.[13,14]

Artists showed every aspect of war, battle and combat. Vases depict dogs and birds eating the dead, warriors dancing with severed heads, the murder of children and the capture and rape of their mothers. They also established the canon for most of western art in the round.

The Romans employed Greek artists, commissioned copies and imitated Greek art, but they had their own particular way of celebrating victory. The victorious general sponsored a parade – the triumph – featuring the prisoners of war (some of whom would be executed after the triumph while others would fight in the arena or labour in the mines), the victorious soldiers, the loot from the campaign, painted placards with scenes from the war and, as the culminating figure, the victorious commander drawn in a chariot with a victory wreath held over his head and a slave murmuring in his ear, *remember you are human.* He would pass through a victory or triumphal arch; a temporary construction at first but, under the empire, built of stone to be a permanent commemoration of the emperors' victories. Thus the Arch of Titus shows a famous triumphal scene of Roman soldiers carrying a menorah from the temple of Jerusalem. Needless to say, the triumphal arch has been imitated and repeated in modern times.[15] American soldiers paraded past the Arc de Triomphe in 1944 where German soldiers had paraded before them – and, before them, the Allies in 1919.

Trajan, to commemorate his victory over the Dacians, commissioned a column (Trajan's Column), dedicated in the forum of Trajan in January AD 112. The column including its base is 125 feet high; the relief, if unwound, would be about 656 feet long. Whether it was intended to be an actual record of events of the two wars, a kind of physical representation of his *Commentaries,* or a general artistic impression is subject to argument but, in either case, the column is a magnificent record of the Roman army in action: advancing, cutting its way through forests, building roads, bridging rivers and fortifying camps – the legionnaires did the actual construction while the auxiliaries stood guard. It depicts details of the personal equipment, arms and armour of the legions, the auxiliaries and the allies. There are scenes that must have been well known incidents at the time – a drunken Dacian falling off a mule, for example – but for which we have no explanation.

As with Trajan's Column, the Column of Marcus Aurelius presents scenes from his campaigns; in this case, against the Germans. We do not know the artistic purpose of different scenes. For example, one scene depicts a female captive with her child clinging to her – were the spectators supposed to feel the pathos of war or just see sex and profit?

And, of course, both the Greeks and Romans honoured their war dead. In the *Iliad*, the heroes receive an individual barrow, the common soldiers a common barrow. (The melancholy truth is that the gods will wipe away those barrows as though they never were.) The barrow over the Athenian dead at Marathon still exists, tombstones of a few individual Athenians survive and a very few commemorating Spartans who died 'in war'. One individual, private monument in Athens represents a grieving hoplite sitting beside his shield and helmet on the edge of the sea. (Apparently he died abroad or was lost at sea.)[16] States honoured their citizen heroes in state ceremonies, and the Athenians had a public funeral at which a prominent

Athenian would speak. The most famous such address is Thucydides' account of the speech of Pericles. The funeral address also continues into our own time, for example the Gettysburg address. A nation of citizen-soldiers must honour its fallen.

Those who died in combat, if at all possible, were washed – particularly their wounds – and laid out in their armour (in Homeric times) or a simple military cloak (in Sparta).[17] In Athens, those who died at Plataea and Marathon received special, common burial on the spot and were honoured with annual rites but, otherwise, memorials to the dead were placed along a street on which pedestrians would continually be reminded of the heroic sacrifice.[18] The Athenians inscribed annual lists of those who died in war. In Sparta, only those killed in action had named markers. If a number of citizens were killed on foreign service, they would be cremated separately and their ashes brought to their families. Those in common graves might receive an annual meal, as the dead at Plataea were offered a black bull.[19] The State put up some monuments, others were produced by family survivors.

One of the common symbols of the courageous dead was the lion. It marked the graves of the Sacred Band of Thebes at Charonea and also the individual tomb: it was the royal symbol and the symbol of power and savagery.[20] All of these monuments and works of art are a physical legacy which we can visit, examine and touch. The lion remained a powerful symbol throughout history – a grieving lion commemorates the Swiss guards who died protecting Marie Antoinette.

We continue to honour the war dead in ways which are a direct imitation of the Greeks and Romans, with memorials which reflect classical architecture and figural themes. However, we also have new technology with which to record combat and, with the new technology, new questions about the appropriateness of pictures of the dead and wounded. (Greeks tended to show the death of soldiers, even barbarians, as a sort of falling asleep.)

The first known photograph (a daguerreotype) of a scene of war was taken in 1847 in Saltillo, Mexico of the battlefield of Buena Vista.[21] The first known photographer to take pictures of troops at war was the Englishman, Robert Fenton, during the Crimean War (1855). Between 1856 and 1871 American and European military services established photographic schools, appointed official photographers and experimented with photography, including aerial photography, for use in combat. By the end of the nineteenth century, photographers were using celluloid films in place of glass plates.

The American Civil War (1861–5) was the first war to be documented extensively with photographs (although the most famous photographer Matthew Brady – who was given a succinct note by President Lincoln, 'Pass Brady!' – had to pay his own expenses). The photographs had a diminished public impact because newspapers were unable to reproduce them. Due to the nature of the photographic process then – the slow exposure – Brady did not take 'combat action' photos.

By the time of the Indian wars and then the Spanish–American war (1898) photographers were taking real combat photographs: one in the Spanish–American war, for instance, shows American soldiers under fire. By World War I, combat photography was well established and the motion picture was introduced. Aerial observation and photography was promoted, so that all the belligerent powers competed to produce one type of aeroplane to observe and photograph the other side, and another type of aeroplane to shoot the first one down.

Since then, it has become established that the different services will send cameramen into the field and that the media, too, will have access. As technology has developed with lighter cameras, and more individual soldiers have the ability to record their surroundings and experiences (beginning with World War I), images of war are sent through private as well as public and military conduits and can be transmitted today almost instantaneously.[22]

Matthew Brady and other Civil War photographers took many photos of the battlefield after the battle, rearranging the dead for a better composition. The dead in many cases appear in fine enough detail that they could have been identified by relatives. In the early days of World War I, British newsreels showed assaults in which British soldiers were killed.

Over time the censors attempted to control the images for purposes of morale as well as to deny the enemy any useful intelligence. In World War II, the decision to show American dead was made at the highest level by President Roosevelt with the proviso that the photos not show the faces or any identifying marks. The purpose was to let the public know there was a real cost to the war.

Photographers in World War II and the Korean War wanted to depict the realities of war, the ugliness and brutality, the starkness and destruction, although they admitted that a person had to experience it to really understand it.[23] (In ancient Greece the audience would have comprised men who had all, or almost all, been there.) As some photographers indicated, they hoped that by presenting the horrors of war they could prevent future wars.[24]

The prevalence of images have given rise to many documentaries based on the photographs of the Civil War, World Wars I and II, and the current conflicts. Every individual now is a potential photographer of stills and video. Some producers, in imitation of modern war documentaries, have created 'ancient' documentaries with a combination of game animation and live actors, simulating on-the-battlefield documentaries of ancient warfare.

The History Channel produces popular films and videos both as individual programmes and as series. Some of the best (available on DVD) are:

Michael Woods, *In the Footsteps of Alexander the Great*, which follows Alexander's route from Macedonia to India; *Warrior Challenge Rome*, where several British and American servicemen and policemen live as Roman legionaries on Hadrian's Wall, train with Roman weapons, dress in Roman costume and go through drills. They live in a Roman barracks, eat Roman food, and then test their acquired skills. (PBS Home Video);*Roman War Machine* (in four parts, History Channel) is the history of the Roman army; *Foot Soldier: The Greeks* and also *The Romans* (A&E Home Video) are entertaining introductions to Greek and Roman armies.

There are series of varying quality analysing ancient battles; one series features a green beret who visits or recreates warrior societies. Others are

The Spartans (PBS Home Video, Bettany Hughes 2004); *Decisive Battles of the Ancient World*, The History Channel, 2006, A&E Television Networks (Thermopylae); *Battles BC*, The History Channel, Four in Hand Entertainment Group, Inc. Season One; *Ancient Greece: Gods and Battles*, A&E Television Networks, LLC. The History Channel. 2010, with programmes such as *Last Stand of the 300*; *Decisive Battles: Marathon, Thermopylae*; *Troy: The Passion of Helen*; *Battles BC: Judgment Day at Marathon*; and *Alexander, Lord of War*.

Then there are more ambitious productions for television networks such as *Rome* and *Spartacus* and films for theatres such as *300*, *Troy*, and *Alexander the Great*.

In addition, groups in the United States and Europe form units of Roman soldiers and reenact camping and battles. One of the organisations is Legio XX, based in Washington, DC. It was founded in 1991 'to recreate the soldiers of the Roman Army for public demonstrations and living history displays'. (www.larp.com.legioxx). The Vexillatio Legionis XIIII Gemina Martia Victrix (The Roman Military Research Society) is based in Coventry, England. (www.romanarmy.net). These are both based on first century AD Roman legions. Fectio Links (www.fectio.org.uk/links.htm) lists similar organisations in the UK, Germany, Netherlands, Spain, France, Italy, Poland and Switzerland.

There are numerous graphic novels set in ancient times. *Age of Bronze: A Thousand Ships* by Eric Shanower is the first of a series of graphic novels retelling the whole story of the Trojan War, and, of course, there is the popular *300*.

There are several series of picture books on ancient armies and weapons, such as *Plataea 479 BC: The Most Glorious Victory Ever Seen* by William Shepherd and Peter Dennis. The Osprey series includes titles like *Marathon 490 BC*, *The Spartan Army*, *Ancient Siege Warfare*, etc. *Plataea*, for example, is 96 pages long, has four double-page illustrations (much like a graphic novel), one double-page illustration of the battlefield, five full-page illustrations and 74 other illustrations.

There are also video games: *Age of Empires* (Microsoft), *Rome: Total*

War (Activision), *Asterix at the Olympic Games* (Atari), *God of War: Ghost of Sparta* (Playstation) and games featuring Alexander the Great, Julius Caesar and the Spartans.

Cartoons, specifically anti-war cartoons and drawings from 1500 to the present, repeat the same themes: war is death and destruction,[25] war devours people,[26] war is fire, ruin, rape, theft, and murder of the innocent victims, women and children,[27] and all for the profit of a few.[28]

Modern cartoonists include new weapons of war – the aeroplane as death,[29] poison gas,[30] the mushroom cloud,[31] and the possibility of total destruction,[32] – but they still represent war in classical form. One cartoonist, for example, draws a classic equestrian statue (celebrating a victorious general, or emperor), but the horse is a skeleton and the figure is a fat pig sporting a wreath.[33] Another draws a classical base and a wreathed figure on top – skeletal Death.[34] The figure of Peace or Victory, wearing a wreath, variously tries to hold back War (represented as Mars) or weeps at the sight of a battlefield.[35]

War is commonly represented either by the Four Horsemen of the Apocalypse or by the bestial god of war – Mars (or Ares) – striding across the field of battle, leaving death, destruction and the victims of atrocities behind him, or driving a tank over a little dove of peace.[36] Mars in Roman armour, as 'magician' Mars, transforms a dove into a skull;[37] plows battlefields with famine; rings church bells shaped like cannon;[38] sells human corpses across a butcher's counter to his customer, Death;[39] shovels cannon fodder into the mouth of the cannon;[40] and, as a large exuberant boy, bangs the drum of war.[41]

As with every other 'legacy', some images (for example, the Siphnian Treasury, the Column of Trajan, the Chigi Vase) survive from all periods of classical antiquity, some – like the Arch of Constantine – inspired imitation by those who wanted to memorialise their own achievements with the patina of antiquity, and some simply inspired by their beauty and skill. The images evolved into a physical expression which an audience would immediately recognise – Mars as war, for example.

Where there is no direct line from the ancient depictions of war to the modern – photography, for instance – antiquity still furnishes a baseline against which to define change, and similarity, in attitude as well as technology. In addition, modern technology is used to portray antiquity in new ways. The wars of antiquity through film, illustration, video games and reenactments are enjoying a vibrant second life.

CONCLUSION

Today we enjoy a rich and varied legacy from Greece and Rome. We have actual survivals (ruins, implements, literature and art – we can hold a shield held by a Spartan at the battle of Sphacteria more than 2,400 years ago, we can see depictions of Roman soldiers in action and we can read a papyrus written in the ancient world or a work transmitted, copy by copy, through the millennia). Writers, artists and motion picture studios have drawn on the classical age for inspiration.

The legacy of ancient war is clear in our understanding of what war is, in our discussions of the morality of war, and in the way we describe war in literature and art, but one question remains – does the experience of war so long ago as expressed in ancient literature still have direct, current and appropriate lessons for us today?

When I returned from Vietnam and went through my own Post-Traumatic Stress Disorder (PTSD) – I did not characterise it as such – I felt that I was isolated, that my experiences were mine alone and my reaction to them unique. In many ways, being home was frightening and disorienting. I drank too much, I felt prone to violence, I couldn't sleep without a loaded revolver at hand, I had nightmares, I couldn't even say the word *Vietnam*. But I did find comfort in the knowledge that I was experiencing what soldiers of 2,800 years earlier had experienced, I did find myself in the *Iliad*. I had felt the grief of Achilles, I had felt the loss of hope and the rage, and I knew men who had ceased to care whether they lived or died, like Achilles after the loss of Patroclus. I found this knowledge reassuring, but I took this reassurance to be personal and without application to anyone else.

However, the plays of Sophocles are being adapted and staged today. A reviewer in the *New York Times* wrote of *These Seven Sicknesses* at the Flea Theater,[1]

> If you're not familiar with the original texts, you may have difficulty imagining how the plays could possibly be staged in isolation, so much do they talk to and build on one another here. They essentially jell into two separate stories: the curse upon the house of the mother-lovin' Oedipus and his descendants, and the Trojan War's psychological, moral, and physical destruction of Greece's finest soldiers and their families.

Another play, *Ajax in Iraq*, compares the experiences of Ajax and a young American woman in Iraq and the consequences of PTSD.[2]

The Defense Department allocates $3.7 million to the Theater of War, which visits military sites throughout the United States to present excerpts from Sophocles' plays *Philoctetes* and *Ajax* to an audience of veterans and their families.[3] One of the actors said, 'These plays are part of a 2,500-year history of mental and emotional pain for soldiers that runs up to the present day'. Sophocles portrayed the empty Philoctetes betrayed by his comrades and Ajax consumed by anger. The purpose is not to effect a 'cure', nor even to treat, but to provide a platform for discussions about PTSD and an attempt to inform veterans that they are not alone and their situation is not unique to them. The issues in these plays are the same as the issues these modern veterans face and they are amazed, and also reassured, to learn that soldiers of 2,500 years ago suffered the same traumas they do.

They and their families can discuss the material of the plays without having to make direct reference to themselves, and they feel freer to discuss these issues when there are no potential consequences for them – psychiatric treatment can end a professional soldier's career. Greece and Rome can still speak directly to us.

Let the remark of one veteran sum up the legacy of ancient warfare. He said, 'I've been Ajax'.

NOTES

Preface

1 Hermann Diels and Walther Kranz (eds), *Die Fragmente der Vorsokratiker* I, 10th ed. (Berlin, 1961), 22 B53.
2 Alfred S. Bradford, *With Arrow, Sword, and Spear: A History of Warfare in the Ancient World* (Westport, CT, 2001), p. 273.
3 Caroline Alexander, *The War That Killed Achilles* (New York, NY, 2009), p. xiii.

Introduction

1 Hugo Grotius, *On the Law of War and Peace* (LaVergne, TN, 2010), p. 3.
2 *Art Of War: Sun Tzu's Legendary Victory Manual Comes to Life*. A video by Four in Hand Entertainment Group for the History Channel (2009).

Chapter I

1 Anthony Grafton, Glenn W. Most and Salvatore Settis (eds), *The Classical Tradition* (Cambridge, MA, 2010), pp. 451–2.
2 Theatre Review: 'An Iliad', *New York Times*, Arts Section (8 March 2012).
3 The gory details are taken from the following passages in the *Iliad*: XII 160–1, XIII 408–10, IV 446, IV 517–31, V 290–3, XIV 493–6, XII 383–5, XVI 345–50, XIII 567–9, XI 145–7, XVII 125–7.
4 Elizabeth Vandiver, *Stand in the Trench, Achilles: Classical Receptions in British Poetry of the Great War* (Oxford, 2010), pp. 230–1.
5 Plutarch, *Alexander* 16, 20, 27, 45, 58, 63.
6 Alfred S. Bradford, *With Arrow, Sword and Spear: A History of Warfare in the Ancient World* (Westport, CT, 2001), pp. xvii, 18–19.
7 Alfred S. Bradford, *Leonidas and the Kings of Sparta: Mightiest Warriors, Fairest Kingdom* (Santa Barbara, CA, 2011), pp. 41–2; translation of *Iliad* XIII 278–86.

Chapter II

1 This chapter is based largely on my book, *With Arrow, Sword, and Spear*.
2 Bob Brier, *Daily Life of the Ancient Egyptians* (New York, NY, 1999), p. 202.
3 Diodorus Siculus, *Bibliotheca Historica* XV 44.3 states specifically that the hoplite took his name from his shield as the peltast did from his, but some scholars believe that the hoplite derived his name from the 'hopla' (the 'stuff', the panoply).
4 Arrian, *Alexander* II 26.
5 Plutarch, *Alexander* 27.9.
6 Arrian, *Alexander* V 19.
7 Livy, *Ab Urbe Condita* XXI 54.3.
8 Ennius, *Annales*, p. 66 #370.
9 Polybius, *Historiae* III 79.
10 Tacitus, *Agricola* 30, spoken by Calgacus.
11 Suetonius, *Caligula* 30 (line from Accius).
12 Lactantius, *De Mortibus Persecutorum* 44.5; Eusebius *vita Constantini*.

Chapter III

1 For this chapter I relied mainly on the following works: J. F. C. Fuller, *Military History of the Western World*, 3 vols (New York, NY, 1987) [1954–7]; John Keegan, *A History of Warfare* (New York, 1993); Geoffrey Parker, *The Military Revolution: Military Innovation and the Rise of the West, 1500–1800*, 2nd ed. (Cambridge, 1996).
2 Stuart Piggott, *Wagon, Chariot, and Carriage: Symbol and Status in the History of Transport* (New York, NY, 1992), p. 69.
3 John Keegan, *The Face of Battle* (New York, NY, 1976), pp. 79–116.
4 Martin van Creveld, *The Art of War: War and Military Thought* (London, 2005), p. 62.
5 Ibid., p. 56.
6 Kenneth Chase, *Firearms: A Global History to 1700* (Cambridge, 2003), pp. 1–2.
7 Ibid., p. 58.
8 Ibid., p. 59; J. R. Partington, *A History of Greek Fire and Gunpowder* (Baltimore, MD, 1998), pp. 91–7.
9 Christopher Duffy, *Siege Warfare* (London, 1979), pp. 8–9.
10 Keegan, *History of Warfare*, p. 326.
11 John Hale, *Renaissance War Studies* (London, 1998), p. 396.
12 Stephen Morillo, Jeremy Black and Paul Lococo, *War in World History: Society, Technology, and War from Ancient Times to the Present* (New York, NY, 2009), p. 308.
13 William Weir, *Fifty Military Leaders Who Changed the World* (Franklin Lakes, NJ, 2007), pp. 128–9; Morillo et al., *War in World History*, pp. 308–9.
14 Napoleon, *Correspondence*, vol. xxxi, p. 354.

15 Van Creveld, *Art of War*, pp. 68–71.
16 Fuller, *Military History of the Western World*, II, p. 64.
17 G. F. Nicolai, *The Biology of War* (London, 1919), p. 65.
18 Parker, *The Military Revolution*, p. 43.
19 Weir, *Fifty Military Leaders*, p. 131.
20 For Napoleon I draw on David G. Chandler, *The Campaigns of Napoleon* (London, 2002).
21 David Howarth, *The Greek Adventure: Lord Byron and Other Eccentrics in the War of Independence* (London, 1976), pp. 69, 73.
22 Ibid., pp. 219–20, 239–40.
23 Doris Kearns Goodwin, *Team of Rivals* (New York, NY, 2006), Chapter 16, p. 437.
24 Ernst Jünger, *Storm of Steel* (London, 2012), p. 5.
25 Rupert Brooke, 'Peace', in Brian Gardner (ed.), *Up the Line to Death: The War Poets 1914–1918* (London, 1964), p. 10.
26 Oscar Williams, *A Little Treasury of British Poetry* (New York, NY, 1951), p. 704.
27 John Keegan, *Mask of Command* (New York, NY, 1988), p. 235.
28 Michael Burleigh, *Moral Combat: Good and Evil in World War II* (New York, NY, 2011), p. 173.
29 Keegan, *History of Warfare*, p. 374.

Chapter IV

1 Herodotus, *Histories* I 87.
2 Plato, *Laws* 625E–626B.
3 Ibid., 626C.
4 Hesiod, *Works and Days* 109–201.
5 Ibid., 176–8.
6 Ibid., 11–26.
7 Cicero, *de officiis* 1.7.22–3.
8 Ibid., 1.7.20–1.
9 Lucretius, *De Rerum Natura* V 953ff.
10 Ibid., V 961.
11 Ibid., V 962–1030.
12 Aristotle, *Politics* I 2.
13 Cicero, *de republica* 3.23.35.
14 Cicero, *de officiis* 1.11.34–5.
15 Alfred S. Bradford, *Leonidas and the Kings of Sparta: Mightiest Warriors, Fairest Kingdom* (Santa Barbara, CA, 2011), pp. 118–20; Thucydides, *Historiae* I 80–5ff.
16 Bradford, *Leonidas*, pp. 123–4; Thucydides, *Historiae* II 72–4.
17 Cicero, *de off.* 2.5.18.
18 Ibid., 1.11.34–5.
19 Plutarch, *Pericles* 30.1; Aristophanes, *Acharnians* 537.

20 *Acharnians* 524–31.
21 Plato, *Alcibiades* I 108d–109d.
22 Plutarch, *Moralia (apophthegmata Laconica)* 231D2; Bradford, *Leonidas*, p. 6.
23 Thucydides, *Historiae* 6.105.11; Victor Alonso, 'Peace and International Law in Ancient Greece' in Kurt A. Raaflaub (ed.), *War and Peace in the Ancient World* (Hoboken, NJ, 2006).
24 Thucydides, *Historiae* 2.64.
25 Demosthenes, *Orationes* 2 *(Olynthiacs)* 24.
26 Ibid., *Epitaphion* 7–11.
27 Isocrates, *Panegyric* 24, 72, 80, 104–6.
28 Isocrates, *Archidamos.*
29 Polybius, *Historiae* 5.11.3.
30 Dionysius Halicarnassus, *Roman Antiquities* 2.72.3–9.
31 Alfred S. Bradford, *With Arrow, Sword, and Spear: A History of Warfare in the Ancient World* (Westport, CT, 2001), p. 170.
32 Cicero, *on the responses of the haruspices* 9.19.
33 Cicero, *de officiis* 1.11.36; Livy 1.32.5–14; Isidore of Seville, *de republica* III: 18.1
34 Plutarch, *Julius Caesar* 15.
35 *de off.* 2.24.85, 1.11.34–5.
36 *de off.* 1.11.35.
37 *de off.* 2.8.27.
38 Cicero, *pro imperio Cn. Pompeio* (to the people) 2.6.
39 Ambrose of Milan, *On the Duties of the Clergy* 1.34.178, 3.3.23.
40 Ambrose of Milan, *On Jacob* 2.6.29; Louis J. Swift, 'Early Christian Views on War and Peace', in Kurt A. Raaflaub (ed.), *War and Peace in the Ancient World* (Hoboken, NJ, 2006), pp. 279–96.
41 St Augustine, *De Civitate Dei* 4.15; Doyne Dawson, *The Origins of Western Warfare: Militarism and Morality in the Ancient World* (Boulder, CO, 1998), pp. 171–2.
42 Gratian, *Decretum Gratiani*, Canon Law causa 23; Dawson, *Western Warfare*, p. 173.
43 Thomas Aquinas, *Summa Theologiae* 2.2 quaestio 40; Dawson, *Western Warfare*, pp. 174–5.
44 Dawson, *Western Warfare*, pp. 176–7.
45 Martin van Creveld, *The Art of War: War and Military Thought* (London, 2005), p. 54.
46 'Brief discourse of Warre' in Geoffrey Parker, *The Military Revolution: Military Innovation and the Rise of the West, 1500–1800*, 2nd ed. (Cambridge, 1996), p. 6.
47 Van Creveld, *Art of War*, p. 73.
48 Gentili, 'de iure belli' (1588, rev. 1598) in van Creveld, *Art of War*.
49 Cicero, *Philippics* V xi 30–1, Cassius Dio, *Historiae Romanae* XLV 36 1.

50 Tuck 19 from James Spedding (ed.), *The Letters and the Life of Francis Bacon* (London, 1874), p. 477.
51 Dawson, *Western Warfare*, p. 183.
52 Ibid., pp. 184–5.
53 The *New York Times* (Tuesday 28 February 2012) in the Op Ed and Letters section on 'The Question of Intervention in Syria' in reference to 'How to Halt the Butchery in Syria' by Anne-Marie Slaughter, Op Ed, 24 February.
54 Grotius, *Law of War*, Book II Chapter I summary.
55 Ibid., p. 214.
56 Richard Tuck, *The Rights of War and Peace: Political Thought and the International Order from Grotius to Kant*, repr. 2009 (Oxford, 1999).
57 Ibid., p. 15.
58 Ibid., p. 6.
59 Ibid., p. 228.
60 Ibid., p. 105.
61 Thomas Hobbes, *Leviathan* (1651), pt. 1, Chapter 13.
62 Baruch Spinoza, trans. Jonathan Israel and Michael Silverthorne, *Tractatus Politicus*, 1677 (Cambridge, 2007), Ch. 5, Section 3.
63 Gregory Reichberg, Henrik Syse and Endre Begby (eds), *The Ethics of War: Classic and Contemporary Readings* (Malden, MA, 2006), p. 482.
64 Ibid., p. 483.
65 Ibid., p. 488.
66 Ibid., p. 481.
67 Ibid., pp. 520–1.
68 Ardrey, African Genesis, p. 11.
69 Napoleon A. Chagnon, *Noble Savages* (New York, NY, 2013), pp. 232, 384.
70 Aron in Lawrence Freedman (ed.), *War* (Oxford 1994), pp. 77–80.
71 Interview: www.boreme.com/posting.php?id=31736#.UlwlBZ15mK0. Interview of Jane Goodall, December 9, 1997.
72 Nicholas Wade, 'Chimps, too, wage war and annex rival territory', *New York Times* (21 June 2010), *Science Times*.
73 Reichberg et al., *Ethics of War*, pp. 454–74 for a thorough discussion of these three and excerpts from their writing.
74 Ibid., pp. 504–17.
75 Ibid., pp. 475–9.
76 Michael Burleigh, *Moral Combat: Good and Evil in World War II* (New York, NY, 2011), p. 258.
77 Found in Reichberg et al., *Ethics of War*, pp. 574–85.
78 Ibid., p. 585.
79 Ibid., p. 512.
80 John Fabian Witt, *Lincoln's Code: The Laws of War in American History* (New York, NY, 2012), pp. 19–26.
81 Ibid., p. 65, quoting John Reid.

82 I Ch I, 2. Definition. Can be found in Reichberg et al., *Ethics of War*. p. 554.

83 Can be found in Reichberg et al., *Ethics of War*, p. 556.

84 Witt, *Lincoln's Code*, p. 177.

85 Reichberg et al., *Ethics of War*, p. 568.

86 W. Michael Reisman and Chris T. Antoniou (eds), *The Laws of War: A Comprehensive Collection of Primary Documents on International Laws Governing Armed Conflict* (New York, NY, 1994), p. 35.

87 11 August 1880, reported by Lloyd Lewis in *Sherman, Fighting Prophet* (1932). Cited in Elizabeth Knowles (ed.), *Oxford Dictionary of Quotations* (Oxford, 2004), p. 734, quotation #17.

88 Burleigh, *Moral Combat*, pp. 510–11.

89 Ibid., p. 513.

90 Ibid., p. 516.

91 Ibid., pp. 528–9.

92 Ibid., p. 175.

93 Cicero, *pro Milone* 11: *silent enim leges inter armes.*

94 Author's recollection.

95 James Turner Johnson (b. 1938) in Reichberg et al., *Ethics of War*, p. 662.

Chapter V

1 Alfred S. Bradford, *With Arrow, Sword, and Spear: A History of Warfare in the Ancient World* (Westport, CT, 2001), pp. 9–11.

2 Martin van Creveld, *The Art of War: War and Military Thought* (London, 2005), p. 29.

3 1 Kings [Samuel] 4.1–2.

4 Ibid., 4.10.

5 Ibid., 17.4–7.

6 Ibid., 17.48–52.

7 Ibid., 17.45.

8 Gilbert Murray et al. (eds), *Oxford Book of Greek Verse* (Oxford, 1966) #97.

9 Ibid., ##103–13.

10 Alfred S. Bradford, *Some Even Volunteered: The First Wolfhounds Pacify Vietnam* (Westport, CT, 1994), p. 183.

11 Herodotus, *Histories* IX 54–6.

12 Ibid., IX 72.

13 Thucydides, *Historiae* I 22.

14 Ibid., VII 50.4.

15 Ibid., V 66.2.

16 Ibid., V 68.2–3.

17 Victor Davis Hanson, *Ripples of Battle: How the Wars of the Past Still Determine How We Fight, How We Live, and How We Think* (New York, NY, 2003), pp. 232–8: 'The Birth of Tactics'.

18 Ibid., p. 44.
19 Xenophon, *Hellenica* VII 22.
20 Polybius, *Historiae* XII 25e.
21 Ibid., I 14.6.
22 Ibid., IX 1–2, I 1.2.
23 Arrian, *Alexander* III 10.1–2.
24 Livy, *Ab Urbe Condita* XXII 7.8.
25 Ibid., XXII 44.
26 Ibid., XXII 51.5–9.
27 Tacitus, *Histories* I 22.
28 Ibid., I 29.
29 Ibid., I 36.3.
30 Ibid., I 39.
31 Ibid., I 49.4.
32 Ibid., III 21–31.
33 Ammianus Marcellinus, *Roman Histories* XXXI 13.3.
34 Ibid., XXXI 13.11. Ammianus also gives a vivid eyewitness account of the siege of Amida at XIX 1–8.7.
35 Judith Barrington, *Writing the Memoir: From Truth to Art*, 2nd ed. (Portland, OR, 2002), pp. 21–3, 27, 55, 95.
36 Xenophon, *Anabasis* IV 5.25–6.
37 John Keegan, *The Face of Battle* (New York, NY, 1976), pp. 63–4.
38 Caesar, *Gallic Wars* II 25.
39 Josephus, *Jewish War* III 15 (193–6).
40 Ibid., III viii 3 (350–2).
41 Yuval Noah Harari, *Renaissance Military Memoirs: War, History, and Identity, 1450–1600* (Rochester, NY, 2004), p. 188.
42 Plutarch, *Aratus* 3.3, 38.6.
43 Harari, *Renaissance Military Memoirs*, p. 191.
44 Ibid., pp. 193–5.
45 Ibid., and Yuval Noah Harari, 'Military memoirs: a historical overview of the genre from the Middle Ages to the Late Modern Era', *War in History*, 14, 3 (2007), pp. 289–309.
46 Harari, *Renaissance Military Memoirs*, p. 190.
47 Ibid., p. xxxiii.
48 Ibid., pp. 78–9.
49 Thucydides, *Historiae* I.22.
50 Guillaume Cretin in Harari, *Renaissance Military Memoirs*, p. 83.
51 Herman Wouk, *The Caine Mutiny* (Franklin Center, PA, 1978), p. 258.
52 Arrian, *Alexander* II 3–9.
53 Ibid., II 10.2.
54 Harari, *Renaissance Military Memoirs*, pp. 298–9.
55 Elizabeth Vandiver, *Stand in the Trench, Achilles: Classical Receptions in British Poetry of the Great War* (Oxford, 2010), pp. 64–5.

56 Ibid., pp. 71–2; Erich Maria Remarque, *All Quiet on the Western Front* (Boston, MA, 1929), pp. 20–1.

57 Vandiver, summary, p. 162; Remarque, *All Quiet*, p. 21.

58 Cornelius Ryan, *The Longest Day* (New York, NY, 1959), p. 8.

Chapter VI

1 Alfred S. Bradford, *With Arrow, Sword, and Spear: A History of Warfare in the Ancient World* (Westport, CT, 2001), p. xix.

2 Ibid., pp. 3–8, xix.

3 Ibid., p. xvii.

4 Peter Connolly, *Greece and Rome at War* (Eaglewood Cliffs, NJ, 1981), pp. 38–9; P. E. Arias and Max Hirmer, *Greek Vase Painting* (New York, NY, c.1960) #16 and IV detail.

5 Arias, *Greek Vase Painting*, #48.

6 Ibid., #193.

7 Ibid., #125.

8 Ibid., #145.

9 Alfred S. Bradford, *Leonidas and the Kings of Sparta: Mightiest Warriors, Fairest Kingdom* (Santa Barbara, CA, 2011), p. 52.

10 Pausanias, *Graeciae Descriptio* I xv.

11 John Warry, *Warfare in the Classical World* (Norman, OK, 1995), p. 70.

12 Reinhard Lullies and Max Hirmer, *Greek Sculpture* (New York, NY, 1960), ##48–55.

13 Ibid., ## 232–7.

14 Ibid., ## 251–9.

15 Charles Eugene Sumners, *Darkness Visible: Memoir of a World War II Combat Photographer* (Jefferson, NC, 2002), p. 60.

16 Bradford, *With Arrow*, p. 78.

17 Robert Garland, *The Greek Way of Death*, 2nd ed. (Ithaca, NY, 2001), pp. 24–5.

18 Ibid., p. 89f.

19 Ibid., p. 113.

20 Emily Vermeule, *Aspects of Death in Early Greek Art and Poetry* (Berkeley, CA, 1979), p. 89, fig. 8.

21 Norman B. Moyes, *Battle Eye: A History of American Combat Photography* (New York, NY, 1996), p. 142.

22 Sumners, *Darkness Visible*, p. 31.

23 Susan D. Moeller, *Shooting War: Photography and the American Experience of Combat* (New York, NY, 1989), p. 52.

24 Ibid., p. 210.

25 Craig Yoe, *The Great Anti-War Cartoons* (Seattle, WA, 2009), p. 56, Hans Sebald Beham (1520).

26 Ibid., p. 36, Anonymous, Germany (1600s).

27 Ibid., p. 69 (1915).
28 Ibid., p. 46, Peter Bruegel the Elder, 'The Fight of the Money-Bags and Strong Boxes'.
29 Ibid., p. 78–9, Anonymous, France (1914).
30 Ibid., p. 128, Willibald Krain, parent and children in gas masks (1915).
31 Ibid., p. 85, Robert Osborn (1946).
32 Ibid., p. 8, Giuseppe Sacharini, the skeleton of war devouring the skeleton of fame which in turn is devouring war (1916).
33 Ibid., p. 61.
34 Ibid., p. 161.
35 Ibid., p. 183, Sir John Tenniel, Peace/victory (1862); p. 181, Walter Crane, peace overcoming war (1906); p. 171, peace holding back war.
36 Ibid., p. 179, an imitation shows Franklin Roosevelt instead of the dove (1938).
37 Ibid., p. 39.
38 Ibid., p. 42.
39 Ibid., p. 41.
40 Ibid., p. 72 (1939).
41 Ibid., p 105; Mars also appears on pp. 18, 33–5, and elsewhere.

Conclusion

1 Catherine Rampell, 'Adapting Sophocles: "These Seven Sicknesses" at Flea Theater', *New York Times*, Arts Section, p. C2 (4 February 2012).
2 *New York Times* review, Arts Section (8 June 2011).
3 *New York Times*, p. C1 (9 December 2009), New York edition, also discussed at MSNBC in 2008.

Translations of classical texts are the author's own, unless otherwise noted.

BIBLIOGRAPHY

Aeschylus, *Persians*.

Alexander, Caroline, *The War That Killed Achilles* (New York, NY, 2009).

Alonso, Victor, 'Peace and International Law in Ancient Greece' in Kurt A. Raaflaub (ed.), *War and Peace in the Ancient World* (Hoboken, NJ, 2006).

Ambrose of Milan (St Ambrose), *On the Duties of the Clergy*.

——— *On Jacob*.

Ammianus Marcellinus, *Roman History*.

Aquinas, Thomas, *Summa Theologiae*.

Ardrey, Robert. *African Genesis*. New York, 1967.

Arias, P. E. and Max Hirmer, *Greek Vase Painting* (New York, NY, *c*.1960).

Aristophanes, *Acharnians*.

Aristotle, *Politics*.

Aron, Raymond, 'Biological and Psychological Roots' in Lawrence Freedman (ed.), *War* (Oxford, 1994), pp. 77–81.

Arrian, *Alexander*.

Art Of War: Sun Tzu's Legendary Victory Manual Comes to Life. A video by Four in Hand Entertainment Group for the History Channel (2009).

Bairnsfather, Bruce, *The Bairnsfather Omnibus: Bullets and Billets and From Mud to Mufti* (North Yorkshire, UK, 2000) [1916, 1919].

Barrington, Judith, *Writing the Memoir: From Truth to Art*, 2nd ed. (Portland, OR, 2002).

Barton, Carlin A., *Roman Honor: The Fire in the Bones* (Berkeley, Los Angeles / London, 2001).

Beard, Mary, *The Roman Triumph* (Cambridge, MA, 2007).

Benet, Stephen Vincent, *John Brown's Body* (New York, NY, 1960).

Blunden, Edmund, *Undertones of War* (Chicago, IL, 2007) [1928].

Bowman, James, *Honor: A History* (New York, NY, 2007).

Bradford, Alfred S., *Some Even Volunteered: The First Wolfhounds Pacify Vietnam* (Westport, CT, 1994).

—— *With Arrow, Sword, and Spear: A History of Warfare in the Ancient World* (Westport, CT, 2001).

—— *Flying the Black Flag: A Brief History of Piracy* (Westport, CT, 2007).

—— *Leonidas and the Kings of Sparta: Mightiest Warriors, Fairest Kingdom* (Santa Barbara, CA, 2011).

Brier, Bob, *Daily Life of the Ancient Egyptians* (New York, NY, 1999).

Brooke, Rupert, *The Collected Poems of Rupert Brooke* (New York, NY, 1965).

Bryant, Mark, *World War I in Cartoons* (London, 2006).

—— *World War II in Cartoons* (London, 2009) [1989].

Bryce, Trevor, *Life and Society in the Hittite World* (Oxford, 2004).

Burleigh, Michael, *Moral Combat: Good and Evil in World War II* (New York, NY, 2011).

Caesar, *Civil War*.

—— *Gallic War*.

Camp, L. Sprague de, *An Elephant for Aristotle* (New York, NY, 1958).

—— *The Ancient Engineers* (New York, NY, 1993).

Cassius Dio, *Historiae Romanae*.

Cato, *Commentaries*.

Chagnon, Napoleon A., *Yanomamö* (Belmont, CA, 2013).

—— *Noble Savages* (New York, NY, 2013).

Chandler, David G., *The Campaigns of Napoleon* (London, 2002).

Chase, Kenneth, *Firearms: A Global History to 1700* (Cambridge, 2003).

Chittenden, Varick A., *Vietnam Remembered: The Folk Art of Marine Combat Veteran Michael D. Cousino, Sr.* (Jackson, MS, 1995).

Cicero, *de officiis*.

—— *de republica*.

—— *on the responses of the haruspices*.

—— *Philippics*.

—— *pro imperio Cn. Pompeio*.

—— *pro Milone*.

Connolly, Peter, *Greece and Rome at War* (Eaglewood Cliffs, NJ, 1981).

Creveld, Martin van, *The Art of War: War and Military Thought* (London, 2005).

Davis, Burke, *Marine! The Life of Chesty Puller* (New York, NY, 1964).

Dawson, Doyne, *The Origins of Western Warfare: Militarism and Morality in the Ancient World* (Boulder, CO, 1998).

Demosthenes, *Orationes*.

Diaz del Castillo, Bernal, *The Discovery and Conquest of Mexico* (New York, NY, 1956).

Diels, Hermann and Walther Kranz (eds), *Die Fragmente der Vorsokratiker* I, 10th ed. (Berlin, 1961).

Diodorus Siculus, *Bibliotheca Historica*.

Dionysius Halicarnassus, *Roman Antiquities*.

Drake, David, *Ranks of Bronze* (Wake Forest, NC, 2001).

Duffy, Christopher, *Siege Warfare* (London, 1979).

Duggan, Alfred, *Winter Quarters* (London, 2012).

Eiserman, Major Frederick A., *War on Film: Military History Education: Video Tapes, Motion Pictures, and Related Audiovisual Aids*, Historical Bibliography No. 6 (Fort Leavenworth, KS, 1987).

Ennius, *Annales*.

—— *Poesis Reliquiae*, ed. Johann Vahlen (Amsterdam, 1967).

Eusebius, *vita Constantini*.

Fields, Nic and Brian Delf (illus.), *Ancient Greek Fortifications 500–300 BC* (Oxford, 2006).

Fliess, Peter, 'War Guilt in the History of Thucydides', *Traditio*, 16 (1) (1960), pp. 1–17.

Freedman, Lawrence (ed.), *War* (Oxford, 1994).

Fuller, J. F. C., *Military History of the Western World*, 3 vols (New York, NY, 1987) [1954–7].

Fussell, Paul, *The Great War and Modern Memory* (New York, NY, 1975).

Gabriel, Richard A. and Karen S. Metz, *A History of Military Medicine* (New York, NY, 1992).

Gardner, Brian (ed.), *Up the Line to Death: The War Poets 1914–1918* (London, 1964).

Garland, Robert, *The Greek Way of Death*, 2nd ed. (Ithaca, NY, 2001).

Gentili, 'de iure belli' (1588, rev. 1598) in Martin van Creveld, *The Art of War: Wars and Military Thought* (London, 2005).

Gomme, A. W., *A Historical Commentary on Thucydides*, vol. 1 (Oxford, 1956).

Goodwin, Doris Kearns, *Team of Rivals* (New York, NY, 2006).

Grafton, Anthony, Glenn W. Most and Salvatore Settis (eds), *The Classical Tradition* (Cambridge, MA, 2010).

Gratian, *Decretum Gratiani*.

Graves, Robert, *Goodbye to All That* (New York, NY, 1929).

Grotius, Hugo, *On the Law of War and Peace (De iure Belli ac Pacis)* (LaVergne, TN, 2010).

Hackett, Sir John (ed.) and Peter Connolly (illus.), *Warfare in the Ancient World* (New York, NY, 1989).

Hale, John, *Renaissance War Studies* (London, 1988).

Halter, Ed, *From Sun Tzu to Xbox: War and Video Games* (New York, NY, 2006).

Hanson, Victor Davis, *Ripples of Battle: How the Wars of the Past Still Determine How We Fight, How We Live, and How We Think* (New York, NY, 2003).

—— *The Father of Us All: War and History, Ancient and Modern* (New York, NY, 2010).

Harari, Yuval Noah, *Renaissance Military Memoirs: War, History, and Identity, 1450–1600* (Rochester, NY, 2004).

—— 'Military memoirs: a historical overview of the genre from the Middle Ages to the Late Modern Era', *War in History*, 14 (2007), pp. 289–309.

Hedges, Chris, *War Is a Force That Gives Us Meaning* (New York, NY, 2003).

Herodotus, *Histories*.

Hesiod, *Works and Days*.

Hobbes, Thomas, *Leviathan* (Cambridge, 1991).

Holmes, Richard (ed.), *The Oxford Companion to Military History* (Oxford, 2001).

Homer, *Odyssey*.

Homer, *The Iliad*, trans. Stephen Mitchell (New York, NY, 2011).

Howarth, David, *The Greek Adventure: Lord Byron and Other Eccentrics in the War of Independence* (London, 1976).

Immelmann, Frantz, *Immelmann: The Eagle of Lille* (Drexel Hill, PA, 2009).

Isidore of Seville, *de republica*.

Isocrates, *Archidamos*.

—— *Panegyric*.

James, Simon, 'Strategems, combat, and "chemical warfare" in the siege mines of Dura-Europus', *American Journal of Archaeology* (2011), pp. 69–101.

Jessup, Jr., John E. and Robert W. Coakley (eds), *A Guide to the Study and Use of Military History* (Washington, DC, 1979).

Josephus, *Antiquities of the Jews*.

—— *Jewish War*.

Jünger, Ernst, *Storm of Steel* (London, 2012).

Keegan, John, *The Face of Battle* (New York, NY, 1976).

—— *Mask of Command* (New York, NY, 1988).

—— *A History of Warfare* (New York, NY, 1993).

Keren, Michael and Holger H. Herwig (eds), *War Memory and Popular Culture: Essays on Modes of Remembrance and Commemoration* (Jefferson, NC, 2009).

Kilduff, Peter, *Black Fokker Leader: Carl Degelow – The First World War's Last Airfighter Knight* (London, 2009).

Knowles, Elizabeth (ed.), *Oxford Dictionary of Quotations* (Oxford, 2004).

Lactantius, *De Mortibus Persecutorum*.

Law, Bernard (Viscount Montgomery of Alamein), *The Memoirs of Field-Marshal the Viscount Montgomery of Alamein, K. G.* (Cleveland and New York, NY, 1958).

Lepper, Frank and Sheppard Frere, *Trajan's Column* (Wolfboro, NH, 1988).

Lewin, Ronald, *The Chief: Field Marshall Lord Wavell* (New York, NY, 1980).

Lewis, Mark Edward, *Sanctioned Violence in Early China* (Albany, NY, 1990).

—— *The Early Chinese Empires: Qin and Han* (Cambridge, MA, 2007).

Livy, *Ab Urbe Condita*.

Lucretius, *De Rerum Natura*.

Lucy, J. F., *There's a Devil in the Drum* (East Sussex, UK, 1993).

Lullies, Reinhard and Max Hirmer, *Greek Sculpture* (New York, NY, 1960)

Luttwak, E. N., *Strategy: The Logic of War and Peace*, rev. and enlarged ed. (Cambridge, MA, 2001).

McCallum, Jack Edward, *Military Medicine: From Ancient Times to the 21st Century* (Santa Barbara, CA, 2008).

McCullough, Colleen, *First Man in Rome* (London, 2008).

Machiavelli, *Discourses* (New York, NY, 1983).

—— *The Prince* (Amherst, NY, 1986).

—— *Art of War* (Chicago, IL, 1991).

Maddow, Rachel, *Drift: The Unmooring of American Military Power* (New York, NY, 2012).

Majno, Guido, *The Healing Hand: Man and Wound in the Ancient World* (Cambridge, 1975).

Marsland, Elizabeth A., *The Nation's Cause: French, English, and German Poetry of the First World War* (New York, NY, 1991).

Martin, Joseph Plumb, *Ordinary Courage: The Revolutionary War Adventures of Joseph Plumb Martin* (Malden, MA, 2008).

Mattox, John Mark, *Saint Augustine and the Theory of Just War* (New York, NY, 2006).

Mill, John Stuart, 'A few words on non-intervention', in Gregory Reichberg, Henrik Syse and Endre Begby (eds), *The Ethics of War: Classic and Contemporary Readings* (Malden, MA, 2006).

Miller, Frank and Lynne Varley, *300* (Milwaukie, OR, 1999).

Moeller, Susan D., *Shooting War: Photography and the American Experience of Combat* (New York, NY, 1989).

Morillo, Stephen, Jeremy Black and Paul Lococo, *War in World History: Society, Technology, and War from Ancient Times to the Present* (New York, NY, 2009).

Moyes, Norman B., *Battle Eye: A History of American Combat Photography* (New York, NY, 1996).

Murphy, Audie, *To Hell and Back* (New York, NY, 1949).

Murray, Gilbert, et al. (eds.), *Oxford Book of Greek Verse* (Oxford, 1966).

Nicolai, G. F., *The Biology of War* (London, 1919).

Osbourne, Robin, *Archaic and Classical Greek Art* (Oxford, 1998).

Owen, Wilfred, 'Dulce et Decorum Est', in Brian Gardner (ed.), *Up the Line to Death: The War Poets* (London, 1964), pp. 141–2.

Parker, Geoffrey, *The Military Revolution: Military Innovation and the Rise of the West, 1500–1800*, 2nd ed. (Cambridge, 1996).

Partington, J. R., *A History of Greek Fire and Gunpowder* (Baltimore, MD, 1998).

Pausanias, *Graeciae Descriptio*.

Peters, Edward (ed.), *The First Crusade: The Chronicle of Fulcher of Chartres and Other Source Materials*, 2nd ed. (Philadelphia, PA, 1998).

Piggott, Stuart, *Wagon, Chariot, and Carriage: Symbol and Status in the History of Transport* (New York, NY, 1992).

Plato, *Alcibiades*.

—— *Laws*.

Plutarch, *Alexander*.

—— *Aratus*

—— *Julius Caesar*.

—— *Moralia (apophthegmata Laconica)*.

—— *Pericles*.

Polybius, *Historiae*.

Pressfield, Stephen, *Gates of Fire* (New York, NY, 1998).

—— *The Afghan Campaign* (New York, NY, 2006).

Preston, Richard A., Alex Roland and Sydney F. Wise, *Men in Combat: A History of Warfare and its Interrelationships with Western Society* (New York, NY, 1991).

Raaflaub, Kurt (ed.), *War and Peace in the Ancient World* (Hoboken, NJ, 2006).

Rampell, Catherine, 'Adapting Sophocles: "These Seven Sicknesses" at Flea Theater', *The New York Times, The Arts,* p. C2 (4 February 2012).

Ramsey, Neil, *The Military Memoir and Romantic Literary Culture, 1780–1835* (Burlington, VT, 2011).

Reichberg, Gregory, Henrik Syse and Endre Begby (eds), *The Ethics of War: Classic and Contemporary Readings* (Malden, MA, 2006).

Reisman, W. Michael and Chris T. Antoniou (eds), *The Laws of War: A Comprehensive Collection of Primary Documents on International Laws Governing Armed Conflict* (New York, NY, 1994).

Remarque, Erich Maria, *All Quiet on the Western Front* (Boston, MA, 1929).

Renault, Mary, *The Persian Boy* (New York, NY, 1972).

Richards, Frank, *Old Soldiers Never Die* (East Sussex, UK, 2001).

Roy, Pratap Chandra (trans.) and Hiralal Halder (ed.), *The Mahabharata (Bhishma Parva)*, 2nd ed., vol. 5 (Calcutta, 1955–62).

Ryan, Cornelius, *The Longest Day* (New York, NY, 1959).

Sabin, Philip, Hans von Wees and Michael Whitby, *Cambridge History of Greek and Roman Warfare*, 2 vols (Cambridge, 2007).

St Augustine, *De Civitate Dei*.

Sandars, N. K. (trans.), *The Epic of Gilgamesh* (London, 1960).

Sassoon, Siegfried, *Memoirs of a Fox Hunting Man* (New York, NY, 1929).

—— *Memoirs of an Infantry Officer* (London, 1974).

—— *Sherston's Progress* (London, 1974).

Schrader, Helena P., *Leonidas of Sparta: A Boy of the Agoge* (Tucson, AZ, 2010).

Shanower, Eric, *Age of Bronze: A Thousand Ships* (Berkeley, CA, 2001).

Shay, Jonathan, *Achilles in Vietnam: Combat Trauma and the Undoing of Character* (New York, NY, 1994).

Shepherd, William and Peter Dennis (illus.), *Plataea 479 BC: The Most Glorious Victory Ever Seen* (Oxford, 2012).

Sherman, Nancy, *Stoic Warriors: The Ancient Philosophy Behind the Military Mind* (Oxford, 2005).

Sidebottom, Harry, *Warrior of Rome Part One: Fire in the East* (New York, NY, 2009).

Silius Italicus, *Punica*.

Simmons, Dan, *Ilium* (London, 2005).

Spedding, James (ed.), *The Letters and the Life of Francis Bacon* (London, 1874), p. 477.

Spinoza, Baruch, trans. Jonathan Israel and Michael Silverthorne, *Tractatus Politicus*, 1677 (Cambridge, 2007).

Steinbeck, John, *Bombs Away: The Story of a Bomber Team* (New York, NY, 1970) [1942].

—— *Once There Was a War* (New York, NY, 1977) [1943].

Suetonius, *Caligula*.

Sumners, Charles Eugene, *Darkness Visible: Memoir of a World War II Combat Photographer* (Jefferson, NC, 2002).

Sweetenham, Carol (trans.), *Robert the Monk's History of the First Crusade: Historia Iherosolimitana* (Burlington, VT, 2005).

Swift, Louis J., 'Early Christian Views on War and Peace', in Kurt A. Raaflaub (ed.), *War and Peace in the Ancient World* (Hoboken, NJ, 2006).

Syme, Sir Ronald and Anthony R. Birley (ed.), *Roman Papers*, VI (Oxford, 1991).

Tacitus, *Agricola*.

—— *Annals*.

—— *Histories*.

Thucydides, *Historiae*.

Tuck, Richard, *The Rights of War and Peace: Political Thought and the International Order from Grotius to Kant*, repr. 2009 (Oxford, 1999).

Turtledove, Harry, *The Misplaced Legion* (New York, NY, 1987).

Van Buren, Peter, *We Meant Well: How I Helped Lose the Battle for the Hearts and Minds of the Iraqi People* (New York, NY, 2011).

Vandiver, Elizabeth, *Stand in the Trench, Achilles: Classical Receptions in British Poetry of the Great War* (Oxford, 2010).

Vegetius, *de re militari* (or *epitome rei militaris*).

Vermeule, Emily, *Aspects of Death in Early Greek Art and Poetry* (Berkeley, CA, 1979).

Virgil, *Aeneid*.

Wade, Nicholas, 'Chimps, too, wage war and annex rival territory', *New York Times* (21 June 2010), *Science Times*.

Warry, John, *Warfare in the Classical World* (Norman, OK, 1995).

Weir, William, *Fifty Weapons That Changed Warfare* (Franklin Lakes, NJ, 2005).

—— *Fifty Military Leaders Who Changed the World* (Franklin Lakes, NJ, 2007).

Werner, Johannes, *Knight of Germany: Oswald Boelcke, German Ace* (Drexel Hill, PA, 2009).

Williams, Oscar, *A Little Treasury of British Poetry* (New York, NY, 1951).

Williams, Roger, 'Actions of the Lowe Countries, 1618', in Martin van Creveld, *The Art of War: Wars and Military Thought* (London, 2005).

Witt, John Fabian, *Lincoln's Code: The Laws of War in American History* (New York, NY, 2012).

Wolfe, Gene, *Soldier of Arete* (New York, NY, 1989).

Wolfhound Pack, The Newsletter of the 27th Infantry Regiment Historical Society, Spring 2012.

Woodruff, Paul, *The Aias Dilemma: Justice, Fairness, and Rewards* (Oxford, 2011).

Wouk, Herman, *The Caine Mutiny* (Franklin Center, PA, 1978).

Xenophon, *Anabasis*.

—— *Hellenica*.

Yoe, Craig, *The Great Anti-War Cartoons* (Seattle, WA, 2009).

INDEX